Milarepa

Also by Nicole Riggs

Like An Illusion: Lives of the Shangpa Kagyu Masters

Milarepa
Songs on the Spot

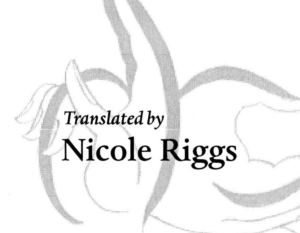

Translated by
Nicole Riggs

Dharma Cloud

E u g e n e · O r e g o n

Published by Dharma Cloud Press
Printed in the United States of America

Cataloging-in-Publication Data

Mi-la-ras-pa, 1040-1123.
    [Songs. English. Selections]
    Milarepa : songs on the spot / translated by Nicole Riggs.
 -- 1st ed.
    p. cm.
    Includes bibliographical references and index.
    LCCN: 2002116247
    ISBN: 0-9705639-3-0

    1. Mi-la-ras-pa, 1040-1123. 2. Lamas--China--Tibet--
Biography--Early works to 1800. 3. Spiritual life--
Buddhism--Early works to 1800. 4. Songs, Tibetan--China
--Tibet. I. Riggs, Nicole. II.Title.

BQ7950.M557 2003   294.3'923'092
                          QBI02-701948

Original cover art: Colman Fockens, Jeffrey Riggs

This book is printed on acid-free paper

Contents

TRANSLATOR'S NOTE

MILAREPA SANG HIS SONGS almost one thousand years ago, but the issues he skillfully raises—the wonders of ordinary awareness, genuineness and the traps of the ego—are more relevant than ever. For these reasons it seemed that he needed to be heard again, in the rhythms of today. I have thus opted for a modern translation which I hope brings to life the clear, vivid voice of Milarepa.

WITH THE AIM of keeping the text fresh and accessible, I have given an approximate phonetic translation of Tibetan names of places, people and deities (except for the deities Tara, *sgrol ma* in Tibetan, and Vajradhara, *rdo rje 'chang* in Tibetan, because conventional usage calls them by their Sanskrit names.) I have also translated as many technical terms as possible, striving for the clearest and most accurate English equivalent. But since a word can have an array of meanings, I have translated the same word in different ways depending on context. Thus the Tibetan *sku* is an honorific word for "body" which I have at times translated as "dimension." Where no satisfactory equivalent exists, I have kept the original technical term, such as *yidam* or *karmamudra*, and given an explanation in the endnotes.

THIS TRANSLATION IS a compilation of nineteen of Milarepa's *Hundred Thousand Songs*, known as *mgur 'bum* in the Tibetan. I selected songs which cover different topics and reveal different sides of Milarepa's personality. The songs are presented in the order that they appear in the original. They were written in an old dialect particular to southwest Tibet, which presented many translation challenges. I referred often to Chang's classic translation, *The Hundred Thousand Songs of Milarepa.* I referred as well to freer translations of some of Milarepa's songs by Khenpo Tsultrim Rinpoche's translators in Pullahari, Nepal.

I'D LIKE TO THANK Lama Wangchen Rinpoche, Keith Dowman, David Curtis, Jeremy Morrelli, John Blay and Jacqueline Medvecka. My love and gratitude to you, Jeff! May all beings realize the luminous nature of reality!

Nicole Riggs
Nevada, USA
January 2003

INTRODUCTION

WANDERING ACROSS THE SNOWY mountains of Tibet and Nepal in the 11th century, the yogi Milarepa cut a unique figure. His skin had turned green after years of subsisting only on nettle soup while meditating in solitude. Having mastered the yogic practice of *tummo* inner heat, he had taken to wearing nothing but a thin cotton loin-cloth summer and winter—earning him the nickname "repa" (literally "man who wears cotton"), which, when his family name was added to it, became "Milarepa."

NOT ONLY WAS HIS appearance eccentric, but Milarepa's songs were also startling: he challenged his listeners with teasing caricatures of their behavior, unveiled the ego-plays behind their thought-patterns, and inspired them with his wisdom and compassion. Shepherds, farmers, landowners, bandits, doctors, young and old, men and women—Milarepa shared the dharma with all of them. Patrons sought out this unconventional yogi as he meditated in natural retreats, asking for his teachings. Sometimes he walked into their homes, appeared at a country inn, a ceremony or a gathering, and burst into songs on the spot. One of the most enduring messages of the great Milarepa, both by personal example and in his songs, is to take all samsaric appearances as the path.

IN "SONGS OF HAPPINESS," Milarepa sings these verses to Teacher Dre:

> The three realms of samsara are magical mansions
> All sentient beings have Buddha nature
> With an instruction pointing out great awareness
> Wherever I stay looks like a castle
> Whomever I meet is a deity
> Whatever I do unfolds in the expanse of reality.

TAKING ALL APPEARANCES as the path means that whatever presents itself is equally a teaching on emptiness so that, for Milarepa, the realms of samsara are like magical mansions. The manifold forms of the universe that arise are not separate from emptiness; they are indistinguishable from it. The notion that appearances are solid and permanent, and the notion that emptiness is nothingness or nihilism, are mere mental constructs.

DEMONIC APPARITIONS TERRIFY those who cling to gross external appearances. In "Demons," however, when Milarepa is presented with demonic forms, he is not afraid because he sees through them—he sees that the "demon" is ultimately a projection of his own mind. Milarepa sings, "To me, the sorcery of demons is just an ornament for the mind! In fact, my bodhichitta only gets stronger." The only demons Milarepa is concerned with are conceptual thoughts, and ultimately, these too are phenomena that arise based on a confluence of causes and conditions. There is nothing intrinsically "demonic" anywhere. In "Duality," Milarepa sings, "Conceptual thoughts are by nature great awareness."

THUS MILAREPA TEACHES that appearances and emptiness are inseparable: appearances arise in dependence upon mind, and mind is empty of inherent existence. Reality experienced this way is at once abysmal because it offers no reference points, and exhilarating because it is constantly changing.

IN "MY WALKING STICK," which Milarepa describes as "a song of symbols," he employs farming as a familiar metaphor to explain to a landowner how, just as farmers plough their fields each spring,

> We, the yogis, sow our fields as well:
> The hard ground of neurotic emotions
> Is fertilized with preliminary practices
> And moistened with the five nectars.

AND IN "SNOW CHALICE," Milarepa sings, "Sheer fear made me build a house / That house is the citadel of emptiness, reality itself / Now I've no fear of collapse!"

A CASUAL READING of this and other similar passages might suggest that Milarepa, in employing external things as metaphors for internal realities, is constructing an inner yogic universe separate from the external one. But in singing what he describes as "symbolic song[s] drawn from absolute reality," he is using common referents to hint at ultimate truth. Such skillful guidance is typical of Milarepa who always adapts his teachings to the needs of his audience. "You're good with worldly farming," he tells the landowner, "we're more into ultimate farming." Later, he explains, "This was an allegorical song, using farming as an example. Be happy, proud man! If you take in this meaning, you'll create much merit."

THE "MEANING" IS THAT which equally pervades samsara and nirvana. Although the ultimate truth of emptiness can't be directly expressed, Milarepa uses conventional metaphors to lead aspirants to it, just as we use a glass to drink water. His own integration of relative and ultimate reality is, in fact, seamless. These metaphors are stepping stones to an ultimate reality that is no different from the conventional, as he demonstrates in "Duality": "In the dharma-body, appearance and emptiness are not two / Samsara and nirvana are experienced as one."

BY COMPARING HIS realized states to ordinary ones ("Like the falling leaves of a palm-tree / Happy is the yoga of no-rebirth."), Milarepa makes those states more accessible to his listeners. Drawing upon things that people readily understand, he challenges them to expand their realization, thus skillfully leading them to liberation—the mark of a Bodhisattva.

I

DEMONS

_____

Namo guru!

JETSUN MILAREPA THE MIGHTY YOGI was staying in a cave at Treasure Grove. He thought to himself, *I should go meditate in the snowy mountains, that's what my Lama advised,* and left for Lashi. He made it to Nyanang, where the locals were celebrating with copious amounts of beer. One of them was saying, "There's this yogi, 'Milarepa,' alive right now. He's an ascetic and he lives all alone in the mountains—quite an exceptional practitioner." More was said along these lines when the Jetsun arrived at their door and was greeted by a young woman covered in jewels. She asked, "Yogi, where do you come from?"

"I'm the great meditator Milarepa. I live in the mountains. Lady, would you kindly offer me food and drink?"

"Of course I'll invite you in, but tell me," the woman continued, "are you really Milarepa?"

"Why should I lie?"

The young woman was delighted and brought him inside. Then she returned to the group of drinkers and announced "That practitioner you were talking about, living far off in the mountains? Well, he's right here at our doorstep." They rushed to the entrance and some prostrated themselves while others asked him all kinds of questions. When they were convinced that this was indeed the Jetsun, they invited him in with the greatest respect and brought out magnificent offerings. They absolutely showered him with their faith and devotion.

THE HOSTESS WITH all the jewels was a rich young girl called Shendormo. She extended every hospitality to the Jetsun and finally asked, "Lama, where are you going?"

"I'm heading for Lashi to meditate."

"Won't you stay at Drelung Kyokmo and spread your blessings here? We'll take care of all your needs."

"A stay at Drelung Kyokmo, the Demons' Plain, would be good for us as much as for you," added local teacher Shakya Guna. "I will be there myself to serve you as best I can."

And a local cattle owner said, "That would be great! You'd make my cattle happy. See, they're all frightened by the demons in the high plain. It's become really unbearable. Oh please, do go there as soon as possible!"

Finally the rest of the party joined in with prostrations. The Jetsun had an answer, "I'll go there, but not because of your cattle. If I go, it's because my Lama commanded me to do so, for practice." This was sufficient for the locals who decided to cook him some fine food and send him off with elaborate preparations. But the Jetsun explained, "I appreciate your attention, but I'm used to solitude and not into big preparations or big groups of people. I'd rather go alone. You can come later."

AND SO THE JETSUN set out alone for the snowy plain. He was hardly at the foot of the mountain when non-human ghosts sprang horrible hallucinations on him. The trail to the mountaintop seemed to vanish into space. Thunder broke out. The mountain itself appeared to shake on all slopes. The river suddenly turned into a raging torrent that flooded both banks and turned the plain into a lake—later famous as Demon Lake. The Jetsun observed all this, made a single movement with his walking stick and all at once the water receded at his feet.

Milarepa was proceeding to the plain when the non-humans shattered both sides of the mountain. An avalanche of huge boulders came crashing down. The Dakini[1] of the Plains formed a sinuous path across the broken slopes—later famous as Dakini Ridge—which helped subdue the smaller ghosts, but the more powerful of the non-human spirits only grew more angry and met together by Dakini Ridge for their next assault.

With a single gaze, the Jetsun overpowered them. All hallucinations dissolved immediately and the shape of Milarepa's foot was imprinted upon the rock. He'd only walked on a little further when the sky cleared. His mind opened up, he settled down—in a place later famous as Hill of Loving-Kindness—and gave birth to the samadhi[2] of great loving-kindness towards all sentient beings. His practice grew in strength and realizations dawned. Afterwards, he moved to the Good-Flow River and practiced the "river-flowing" meditation.

At sunset on the tenth day of fall in the male tiger year, a harmful Nepalese demon called Bharo approached the plain with his formidable ghost army. They crushed the mountain, threatened Milarepa, and aimed their weapons at him.

"We'll tie you up and cut you up!" they hissed, taking on the most hideous shapes. *They're set on hurting me*, thought Milarepa, and he sang this Dharma Song on Cause and Effect:

> Homage to all the Lamas!
> I take refuge in my kind teacher.
> To the eye consciousness, hallucinations of
> Male and female demons take shape, as if from a witches' brew.
> I feel sorry for you hungry ghosts.
> You can't do me harm!
> As a result of bad karma gathered in the past,
> You're now stuck in your bodies and your head-trips,
> Forced to wander through space.
> Your attitude is neurotic and mean-spirited.

And on top of it, your bodies are savage, and your words
   vicious—
"Let's kill him! Let's slaughter him! Let's hit him! Let's
   butcher him!"

But I'm a yogi; I don't do concepts.
I have the view: there is no mind.
In my conduct, I'm brave as a lion.
In my physical body I stick to the fortress of deity-body.
In my words I keep to the palace of the Buddha's speech.
In my mind I hold to the clear-light nature.
The six senses are quite empty of true nature.
That's the kind of yogi I am.
Your evil doesn't phase me.

If the law of cause and effect is true
And results are related to their causes,
You demons are in for a bad rebirth—sorry!
I feel compassion for you, deluded ghosts
Who do not realize this fact.
I, Milarepa the ascetic,
Sing you this dharma song to make you aware.

Of all sentient beings who fill the world,
Not one, not a single one, isn't in some way a relative
Who at one point showed you kindness. Yet suffering awaits
   them all.
So to wish them ill, that's just not smart.
Aren't you better off thinking about cause and effect?
Aren't you better off practicing the ten virtues?
Keep in mind what I said. Think about it.

BUT THE DEMONS were not impressed, "You're not about to brainwash
us with your talk! You won't stop us, we're not letting you go!" And
the demonic army multiplied like magic.

Milarepa took stock of the situation and declared, "By the grace of my Lama, I'm a yogi who's realized the natural state. To me, the sorcery of demons is just an ornament for the mind! In fact, my bodhichitta[3] only gets stronger." And he sang the Song of Seven Great Ornaments:

> I bow at the feet of the translator Marpa.[4]
> I'm a yogi who's realized the natural state,
> And I respond with this Song of Seven Ornaments.
> All you demons gathered here
> Clean your ears, listen carefully!
>
> High on Mount Meru, that great peak,
> Is a shrine glittering with lapis lazuli
> Like an ornament in the sky.
>
> Above the great tree on Mount Meru,
> Sun and moon shine their beams
> Like ornaments over the world.
>
> The *nagas'* miraculous display of bodhichitta
> Sends a rainfall from space
> Like an ornament on the hard earth.
>
> Mist rises from the ocean
> To form clouds
> Like ornaments in the atmosphere.
>
> Sun and moisture meet in summer:
> Rainbows over the meadows
> Like ornaments on the lush hills.
>
> Rainfall from the cold ocean to the west
> Lets the plants of our world blossom
> Like ornaments for all living creatures.

I, the yogi in the mountains,
Meditate on emptiness-mind.
I overpower you, demons,
And make an ornament of your magic.

Listen here, non-human spirits!
Do you know who I am?
In case you don't,
I'm the yogi Milarepa
Deep in my heart, I've given birth to non-conceptual
    bodhichitta
In a clear voice, I've sung you a symbolic song
With true words, I've taught you the dharma
Meaning you good, I've given you my advice.
If you arouse the supreme mind of enlightenment
Then even if you don't actually benefit others
Still, by giving up the ten evils,
You'll gain liberation, peace and happiness.
Listen to my words, lead a meaningful life.
There's happiness ahead if you practice dharma now.

THIS SONG STIRRED devotion for the Jetsun in most of the non-humans. Their conjurations stopped and their tone changed, "Great yogi, wonderful yogi! We wouldn't have understood without your symbolic song. You'll have no more trouble from us. You were kind to teach us about cause and effect. Truth is, we've got bad habits, we're pretty thick, and we basically don't get it. Would you kindly give us a few words full of meaning but easy to understand?" So Milarepa sang the Song of Being:

I bow at your feet, Marpa the translator!
Grant your blessings that I may perfect my bodhichitta.

If you don't connect with these words of true dharma,
This song is nothing but pretty sound.

If my examples aren't congruent with the dharma,
My poem is nothing more than nice verse.

If you don't practice the dharma,
Your so-called knowledge is nothing but sophistry.

If you don't meditate on the essential ear-whispered instruc-
    tions,
Your isolation is nothing more than self-torture.

If you don't engage in the dharma that brings true benefit,
Your work is nothing but hard labor.

If you don't pay close attention to cause and effect,
Your talk is nothing more than wishful thinking.

If you don't practice both the words and their meaning,
Your subtle explanations are nothing but hypocrisy.

Give up evil deeds and you'll feel lighter.
Practice virtue and you'll be stronger.
Put this into practice.

Too many words—that's no good,
Just practice the true meaning as I explained.

THE DEMONS LISTENED with increasing faith. When Milarepa had finished singing, they prostrated themselves, circumambulated and returned home. But the leader, Bharo, along with a small entourage,
continued his hallucinatory display. So the Jetsun Milarepa sang this
new Song about Cause and Effect:

Homage at the feet of kind Marpa.
Non-humans, you listen now!
Your bodies fly through space easily,

But your minds are rigid with evil tendencies.
Neurotics, you dig your fangs into others
But your cruelty will come back to haunt you.
The law of karma always comes around,
There's no way you can avoid it.

I feel for you, confused demons—
You've caused so much harm.
The evil you've done has a terrible force—
Enough to make a person cry.

You're so used to doing evil
That you even get off from killing.
You're so obsessed with taking life
That eating flesh and drinking blood turns you on.

The karmic result of killing other beings
Means that you're reborn as these ghosts.
Your evil deeds have made you fall into a sad state.
What a waste! Change your outlook, turn to the dharma
Practice quickly for a bliss that knows no hope, no fear.

"You're not bad as a scholar going on about the dharma!" sneered
Bharo. "But tell us, from your experience, what makes *you* so confident?" So Milarepa sang the Song of Complete Confidence:

Homage to Marpa, genuine being!
I'm a yogi who's realized the ultimate truth
I gained certainty in the unborn ground
And gradually perfected it on the unobstructed path.
With skillful compassion I now sing
A symbolic song drawn from absolute reality.

The force of your past evil
Prevents you from understanding the ultimate nature,

So I'll sing on the relative plane.
In their flawless sutras and tantras
All omniscient Buddhas of the past
Spoke repeatedly on the topic of cause and effect:
The truth, the undeceiving truth is that
Every sentient being is your relative.

Listen please to my words of loving-kindness.
I'm a yogi who's practiced this in my mindstream
I look at appearances outside, confused and complicated
And know them to be the magical display of unborn mind.
I look at the awareness within
And know it to be empty from the beginning, without a
    fixed foundation.

What leads to realization?
It's the blessings of the Lamas of the lineage,
The qualities gained from solitary meditation
And the transmission of the great Naropa.[5]

I meditated on the correct meaning, the Buddha's meaning
And the tantras, so profoundly skillful, yielded their intent.
My Lama revealed the pith instructions
I meditated steadily on the generation and completion
    stages,[6]
And came to understand dependent arising from deep in-
    side.
Appearances outside, confused and complicated, do not
    frighten me.

I belong to the lineage of the great Saraha[7]
Along with other yogis as numerous as space is vast.
I've practiced and practiced the meaning of mind unadorned
So that confused appearances dissolve into the mental
    sphere.

Study well the dharma texts:
You'll find neither evil nor evil doers—
There's nothing else to get your mind around.

THIS SONG DID IT. Bharo and his demons pledged their very skulls to
Milarepa. They prostrated themselves, circumambulated and promised him a month's worth of supplies. Then they were gone just like
a rainbow. But the next morning at sunrise, they returned with an
entourage adorned with jewels, and presented a variety of brews
including beer and liquor, as well as vessels of long-life elixir and
beautiful dishes of barley and meat. They promised to follow
Milarepa's words and to obey him from that time on. After more
prostrations and circumambulations, they disappeared.

THE EXPERIENCE WAS a boon for Milarepa's practice. His realizations
grew, his body enjoyed the most perfect bliss and he felt no hunger
for a full month. At that point, he thought again of Good-Flow River
and headed there. He came to a vista and settled by a large boulder
that offered shelter. Many dakinis prostrated to him, offering all he
could desire. One of them left two footprints in the rock. Then, like
a rainbow, they vanished.

Milarepa walked on a little further when some non-humans made
a phantasmagoric show of a woman's organs. The Jetsun fixed his
gaze and exposed his own erect penis. Then he concentrated his gaze
once more and displayed nine penises. He conjured a rock in the shape
of a penis and inserted it into an opening in the boulder that was like
a vagina. All hallucinations dissolved. The place became famous as
Nine Passes and Nine Valleys.

Milarepa had now reached the middle of the plain when Bharo
welcomed him with offerings and a request for dharma instructions.
The Jetsun gave him many teachings on cause and effect. At the end,
Bharo dissolved into a huge boulder right in front of Milarepa's teaching seat. For another month, the Jetsun stayed in the middle of the
plain in a happy frame of mind. At that point, he visited his patrons

in Nyanang and told them the story of Drelung Kyokmo, the Demons' Plain. "I've subdued all the demons so it's now a good place
for practice," he explained, instilling faith in his listeners. "In fact, I'd
like to go back there to meditate."

2

CASTLE IN THE SKY

Namo guru!

AFTER HE LEFT RAKMA, the Jetsun Milarepa went to Red Sky Pendant Fortress Cave. One day, a monkey approached. It was riding a rabbit, held a shield of plants, and carried a bow and arrow made of stalks. The Jetsun burst out laughing at the sight.

But the strange creature said with dignity, "I know you were afraid when you first came. If you're no longer afraid, you may go."

"I've gained conviction that all appearances are mind," replied the Jetsun. "And mind itself I know to be dharma-body.[8] But you, demon, can really put on a show! You just crack me up!"

Hearing this, the demon—known as King of Drotang—pledged himself to Milarepa and disappeared in a rainbow.

Later, a group of patrons from Drotang came to see Milarepa. "Tell us, Milarepa, what's so special about this place?" they asked. In response, Milarepa sang the Song of the Castle in the Sky:

> I pray to my holy Lama!
> Do you know what's special about this place?
> In case you don't—
> This is Red Sky Pendant Fortress Cave, a natural retreat.

It's a castle in the sky!
Clouds are dark and thick above
The river clear and blue below
Behind is Red Rock, stark against the sky
And ahead, a patch of bright flowers
At the edge, wild beasts roam and growl
While vultures soar overhead
Sometimes it rains here
And always, the bees buzz
Wild burros run wild
Monkeys fool around
Swallows chirp
Birds of heaven sing sweetly
I hear these rippling sounds
I live with them, they live with me.

There's so much that's special about this place!
Now, I sing you this happy experience song,
An oral instruction hidden between the lines.
All you faithful men and women here today,
Follow my example,
Abandon evil and practice virtue!

AMONG THE PATRONS gathered around Milarepa was a tantric yogi who now asked, "Jetsun, would you kindly give us a teaching on view, meditation and conduct, to celebrate our meeting with you?" In response, Milarepa sang this Song on the Essence of View, Meditation and Conduct:

May the Lama's blessings grace my mind
And help me realize emptiness!

Patrons, here's my response for you,
A song to please the *yidam* deities.[9]

Appearance, emptiness and inseparability—
These three are the essence of the view.

Clear light, no concepts, no distraction—
These three are the essence of meditation.

Completion, no attachment, no grasping—
These three are the essence of conduct.

No hopes, no fears, no illusions—
These three are the essence of fruition.

Not public, not private, not false—
These three are the essence of the *samaya* commitments.[10]

THE PATRONS RETURNED home with renewed faith. In a few days they were back to see how Milarepa was doing. The Jetsun sang them this song:

I bow down at the feet of the holy Lama!
In this solitary forest,
I, Milarepa, meditate happily.

Happy is my stand free of bias
Happy this illusory body free of illness
Happy this practice without sleep
Happy this samadhi without concepts
Happy this inner heat[11] that knows no cold
Happy this practice free of fear
Happy this relaxation free of effort
Happy this solitude free of distractions.
And that's the physical!

Happy is the vehicle of wisdom and skillful means
Happy this practice of generation and completion united

Happy this mindfulness of no coming, no going
Happy this silence away from small talk.
That's the verbal!

Happy is the view free of identification
Happy this meditation that flows free and strong
Happy this conduct free of corruption
Happy this fruition free of hopes and fears.
And that's the mental!

Happy is the clear-light nature, unchanging, non-conceptual
Happy this sphere of pure bliss
Happy my unhindered perceptions.
That's my little song of happiness
Sung straight from experience
Born of the union of view and conduct.
If you're practicing for enlightenment
Put this song into practice!

ONE OF THE LOCALS spoke for them all, "Wonders of body, speech and mind! But how did you get these experiences?"

"They all come from mental realization," replied Milarepa.

"Well, we've never experienced anything like that kind of happiness," said the man. "But just a glimpse would be nice. Please teach us so we can gain realizations." The Jetsun sang the Song of the Twelve Aspects of Mind:

I bow down at the feet of the holy Lama!

Patrons, you want to gain a realization of mind itself;
Here, then, is how you should practice:

Faith, knowledge and discipline,
These three are the life-tree of mind.

Plant it and the path will bloom.
Now that's what I call a tree!

No attachment, no grasping, no delusion,
These three form mind's armor.
Wear them and nothing will hurt you.
Now that's a genuine armor!

Meditation, diligence and tenacity,
These three are the mind's horse.
Ride it and you'll get far.
Now there's a good horse!

Self-awareness, innate clear light, natural bliss,
These three are the fruit of mind.
Sow the seeds, distill the fruit and drink the juice.
Now that's a fruit!

These are the twelve aspects of mind
Sung spontaneously
In answer to your request, dear patrons!

THE PATRONS felt great faith and served Milarepa with the utmost respect. Eventually, the Jetsun decided to move on, and left for Yolmo. This was the story of Milarepa at Red Sky Pendant Fortress Cave.

3

SNOW CHALICE

Namo guru!

THE MIGHTY YOGI Milarepa kept his Lama's injunction to practice by going to Snow Chalice. He was staying in Tiger Cave by Lion Fortress in the forests of Singaling. The local goddess, whom he'd pacified right away, displayed her beautiful form and did wonders at his service.

As Milarepa's practice was deepening, five young nuns came from Mön, asking for dharma teachings, "A frightful place like must present many challenges for practice, Lama, no?"

In praise to the area, Milarepa sang the Song of Giving Birth to Essential Practice:

> I bow down at the feet of the holy Lama!
> Because of good merit, I met a master.
> I've come to a place prophesied by the Lama:
> Under the blissful sky stand the lush mountains of Mön,
> Hills and meadows bursting with flowers,
> Monkeys playing in tall trees—
> A place to run and play!
> A place for birds to sing

To rush, sway, fly away
Rainbows shine dawn to dusk
Summer and winter, the rain falls
Spring and fall, the air is thick with mist.
Girls, it's in this fine, solitary place
That I, the yogi Milarepa, dwell in radiant bliss
Born of meditating that mind is emptiness.
The myriad appearances make me happy
Highs and lows and I'm happy
No bad karma to shape another birth: I'm happy
The manifold confusions—very happy
Terrifying visions make me happy
Free of birth and death and conflicting emotions, I'm happy
Great viciousness and vulgarity, and I'm happy
Untouched by illness—very happy
Pain arises as bliss, I'm happy
Powerful experiential yogas make me very happy
I run, I jump, I dance, I'm happy
Treasure songs of spontaneous words make me happy
When they burst into millions of sounds—very happy
Happy in the spacious confidence of mental strength
Which arises on its own—happy!
Myriad appearances make me happy
This is the happy song of a carefree yogi
For you, so truly devoted!

MILAREPA FOLLOWED THIS SONG with empowerments and oral instructions. Then he entered into meditation and aroused excellent experiences and realizations. With his heart content, he sang this Nectar Song of Oral Instructions:

The Lama, body of enlightenment,
Shows me the path to perfect liberation;
His compassionate activity is the glory of all beings—
He sits on the crown of my head, inseparable from me.

You nuns seated here, you act in accord with the dharma,
You've practiced dharma, your knowledge is good,
Your ways aren't bad,
And you've got the good fortune to meditate on the profound path.

You have the chance to attain enlightenment in a single lifetime,
So don't waste this life getting more attached to your ego!
If you do, you'll only engage in dualities of good and bad,
And if that happens, you'll fall to a low rebirth.

You have the chance to serve the Lama,
So don't grow yourself a big head!
If you do, you'll only turn your teachers against yourselves,
And if that happens, you won't get any mental accomplishments.

You have the chance to guard your samaya vow,
So don't sleep around laypeople!
If you do, you'll only develop evil views,
And if that happens, you'll burn up your pledge.

You have the chance to learn and attend to your studies
So don't get proud over your relative luck!
If you do, you'll only stir up the dying embers of the five poisons,
And if that happens, your good practice will be spoiled.

You have the chance to meditate with others,
So don't get obsessed over who does what!
If you do, you'll only lose track of your practice,
And if that happens, you'll destroy your connection to the dharma.

You have the chance to meditate on the oral instructions for
    the path of means,
So don't go around subduing demons and bestowing bless-
    ings!
If you do, you'll only arouse the demons of your own mind,
And if that happens, you'll fall into spiritual materialism.

You have the chance to arouse experiences and realizations,
So don't run on about your prophecies and clairvoyance!
If you do, you'll only exhaust what must be kept secret,
And if that happens, the signs and qualities on the path will
    be obscured.

Recognize these flaws, give them up!
Commit no evil, eat pure food.
Be scrupulous when you accept offerings,
And don't fawn with phony flattery.
Be humble, and it will all work out.

THE FIVE NUNS wanted to know more. "Please, teach us how to find
our way," said one. In response, the Jetsun Milarepa sang this Song on
Finding One's Way:

Homage to you, kind lord Marpa.
Grant your blessings that I may happily take to heart my
    practice.
You're beginners
Prone to good and evil in this hypocritical place,
Listen to the sublime dharma! Don't waste your chance!
You haven't turned away, you have met with me.
You've gathered much merit, and you're practicing.
So far, so good!
But this isn't enough if you're after mastery.
Here's my intimate advice for achieving your aim,
Given with love. Listen!

When you're settled in your solitary hermitage,
Don't daydream about life down in the village.
If you do, mental demons will lead you astray.
Turn your mind within! You'll surely achieve your aim.

When you persevere in your meditation,
Be mindful that death comes by surprise,
Remember the faults of samsara,
And forget your appetite for the pleasures of this life.
Get ready for hardships! You'll surely achieve your aim.

When you ask for profound meditation instructions,
Don't get a big head about becoming a scholar.
If you do, you'll get caught up in mundane activities,
And if that happens, there's no chance to get out!
Be humble! You'll surely achieve your aim.

When you're arousing all kinds of experiences and realizations,
Don't get puffed up, wanting to show off.
If you do, you'll upset goddesses and dakinis.
Meditate undistracted! You'll surely achieve your aim.

When you accompany your Lama,
Don't start to judge his qualities or defects.
If you do, you'll see nothing but faults.
Keep sacred outlook! You'll surely achieve your aim.

When you're with your dharma brothers and sisters, sitting in rows,
Don't be scheming to get up front like some aging monkey!
If you do, your "want-this, no-want-that" attitude will damage your vows.
Be gracious! You'll surely achieve your aim.

When you're seeking alms in a village,
Don't spin people's heads with deceitful teachings.
If you do, you'll find yourself reborn in the lower realms.
Be honest! You'll surely find your way.

Above all, now and later,
Don't get proud! Don't get vain!
Because if you do, you'll end up a fool both in the dharma
    and in the world.
Give up lies and falsehoods! You'll surely find your way.

The person who has found her way,
Can kindly offer oral instructions
And benefit self and others.
Keep generosity in your heart!

THE SONG INSPIRED the nuns to meditation. All five developed a stronger sense of renunciation towards samsara. Filled with a powerful devotion to the Jetsun, they offered a golden mandala and asked for essential teachings on view, meditation and conduct, which they might put into practice. The Jetsun said, "Use the gold to provide for your practices." And he sang the Song that Nails Down View, Meditation and Conduct:

Great Lama, you've mastered view, meditation and conduct
    front to back—
Grant your blessings that I may dwell in the natural state.

I'll give you three lines on the view.
Three lines on meditation,
Three lines on conduct,
And three lines, too, on fruition.

Three lines on the view:
All worldly appearances are subsumed by mind. Be here!

Be within the clear-light nature of mind itself.
Be without identification!

Three lines on meditation:
Conceptual thoughts are liberated in the dharma-body. Be
    here!
Dwell within the clear-light blissful awareness.
Settle in uncontrived meditative equipoise.

Three lines on conduct:
Virtue? It comes to life spontaneously,
Non-virtue? It's purified in its own ground.
Penance? It can't affect luminous emptiness free of fabrica-
    tion.

Three lines on fruition, too:
There's no nirvana to go to,
There's no samsara to leave behind.
Your own mind *is* the Buddha. Be confident about that!

Within these three-line verses is a single key-point:
Phenomena—the dharma itself—are empty of inherent ex-
    istence.
The gracious, holy Lamas will help you clinch this one.

This could be analyzed a hundred different ways, but that's
    not the idea.
The idea is spontaneous realization.
This is the absolute gem of dharma sayings.

That's the experience of this yogi, which I'm glad to share.
Children, take this to heart!

"So if we're not mistaken," said one, "the basic way to practice is to
ask fervently for blessings from the root Lama. Is there anything

else?" Jetsun was pleased and he replied, "That is indeed the basic way, the root, but there are also branches." And he sang the Song of the Six Guides:

Lama, oral instructions, and disciples
Perseverance, tenacity, and faith
Wisdom, compassion, and nature—
All these flow into the way to practice.

Here are the guides:

This solitary place, away from commotion.
Is the guide that guards my meditation,

The Lama, the adept,
Is the guide that dispels the darkness of ignorance.

Faith (or enthusiasm)
Is the guide that leads to higher rebirths.

The realization of the five faculties[12]
Is the guide that liberates sensory experiences.

The spoken advice of the Kagyu Lamas
Is the guide that teaches the three dimensions.[13]

And there's the triple refuge, rare and sublime.
These are the unerring guides.

These six guides will lead
Yogis and yoginis to the valley of great bliss,
Beyond concepts, beyond fabrications.

Happy is the home of self-knowledge, naturally liberated.
Hold to your definitive understanding,
And stay in solitary places.

This is the thunderous song of a happy yogi!
A rain of sound falls in the ten directions,
The leaves of compassion open,
And the fruit of bodhichitta matures,
All under great clouds of enlightenment!

SEVERAL LOCALS HAD also listened to this song. Now their voices mingled together as each tried to get Milarepa to stay at his or her place. Each one had an argument: Milarepa's samaya was already so strong, or his practice was already so solid, there was no need for him to meditate like a recluse. Also, there were lots of patrons in the area, so perhaps he ought to settle for good. It would be so good if he stayed and turned the wheel of dharma for the benefit of beings . . . The Jetsun now replied, "When I meditate in solitude, I benefit beings. True, my meditation is solid, but great meditators must stick to natural retreats." And he sang this Heart Song:

Oh Lama, I'm grateful to you.
Grant your blessings that my mindstream may mature and
   ripen.
People, you live here, your karma is good, and your practice
   too.
I will respond to your request with a song of oral instruc-
   tions on the profound meaning.
Don't let your attention scatter. Listen carefully!

On this peak, the snow lioness
Sits like an awesome queen
And fears not others.
Confidence is the way of the lioness.

At Red Rock, the vulture, king of birds
Spreads wide his wings
And fears not falling.
Soaring is the way of the vulture.

In the ocean, mother of all rivers, the fish
Swim with agility
And fear not the currents.
Darting, body flashing, is the way of the fish.

In the forests of Mön
Monkeys play
And fear not tumbling.
Playing is the monkeys' way.

Under the canopy of trees
The striped tigress moves with stealth
And fears not the tigers.
Alertness is the way of the tigress.

In the jungles of Singaling
I, Milarepa, meditate on emptiness
And fear not straying from my meditation.
Focus is my way.

In the pure mandala of reality
I practice without distraction
And fear not missing the point.
Staying centered is my way.

In my practice with the physical channels, energy flow and
    seed essence
I avoid blockages.
My dharma is faultless
And let's face it: I get signs real quick.

In self-arising activity
There are lots of ups and downs
But dualistic concepts? None!
It's all auspicious.

In my manipulation of karmic cause and effect—to lead
   beings to maturation—
There seem to be actual occurrences of good and evil,
But meditation gone bad? No!
It's light shed on the particulars of awareness.

All great meditators who hold fast to their meditation
Are uninterested in the world.
Trying to get attention? Not really!
It's an internal goodbye to attachment.

I, the yogi, meditate on the profound path
And take refuge in mountain caves.
I'm not doing it to deceive you,
But because I'm after single-pointed meditation.

Wearing my cotton cloth, I've sung many songs.
Pulling wool over your eyes? Truly not.
Devoted students gathered here,
This deep heart-song is for your benefit!

"YES," SAID ONE, "but it's necessary to have shelter and food if you're
going to meditate in solitude." To this the Jetsun replied, "As for food
and shelter for myself, here's my song—" and he sang the Song of
No Fear:

Father Lama, wish-fulfilling gem, at your feet I bow down!
Grant your blessings so that I may meet with auspicious
   conditions,
That my body may stretch as the palace of deity-body,
That I attain definitive understanding.

Sheer fear made me build a house—
That house is the citadel of emptiness, reality itself.[14]
Now I've no fear of collapse!

Of fear of cold, I got a robe—
That robe is the robe of inner heat.
Now cold doesn't frighten me!

Fear of poverty made me get a jewel—
That jewel is the inexhaustible seven gems.
Now I've no fear of poverty!

Fear of hunger made me look for food—
That food is reality itself, meditation food.
Now I've no fear of hunger!

Of fear of thirst, I sought drink—
That drink is the nectar of mindfulness.
Now thirst doesn't frighten me!

Fear of loneliness led me to companions—
These companions are bliss-emptiness continuous.
Now loneliness doesn't frighten me!

Fear of erring made me find a path—
That path is the great union of wisdom and means.
Now I've no fear of erring!

Wherever I stay, I'm happy!
At Tiger Cave by Lion Fortress in Yolmo
As I hear the tigress' friendly roar
I enter into effortless meditation.
As her cubs play, compassion rises
And I begin an effortless meditation on bodhichitta.
As the monkeys' crazed shrieks ring
I engage in effortless renunciation.
As they clamor with excitement and desire
I engender effortless bodhichitta meditation.

As the sweet, sad sounds of the cuckoo reach me
I can't help but cry.
As I hear the lark's melodious cry
I begin to pay attention.
The various calls of the eagle
Are helpful friends to a yogi's mind.
When I stay in a place like this, I'm happy
Though I've got no companion, I'm still happy.
May this song of a yogi's joy
Clear away the suffering of beings.

THE VILLAGERS WERE so inspired that they swore there and then not to leave the mountain themselves. And in fact all of them stayed, all of them meditated, and all of them attained the ultimate fruition.

ONE DAY, A YIDAM deity told Milarepa to go to the solitudes of Tibet and meditate there for the sake of beings. The yidam deity also prophesied that Milarepa would teach and benefit beings there. Thus the Jetsun headed for Tibet.

4

DUALITY

Namo guru!

AFTER A STAY at White Rock Vajra Fortress Cave, the Jetsun Milarepa settled at Horse Saddle Cave to enhance his practice. A tantric yogi from Kutang, feeling a tremendous faith for the Jetsun, came to see him.

"Lama," said the yogi, "I've meditated for some years, but I don't think I got the point. I've hardly developed any qualities. So would you please give me an oral instruction?"

"Here's everything you need to know—" replied Milarepa. And he sang the Song of Six Essential Points:

> Mental projections way outnumber the dust motes you see
>   in the sunlight;
> A great yogi knows what appears for what it is.
>
> At bottom, the nature of things isn't a product of causes,
>   nor of conditions;
> A great yogi cuts to the core of the issue.
>
> Even a hundred men with spears couldn't stop the thought-
>   bubbles of consciousness;

A great yogi knows not to get fixated on them.

You can't lock up the flow of mind in an iron box;
A great yogi knows mind to be intrinsically empty.

Wisdom gods and goddesses don't say no to sensory plea-
    sures;
A great yogi knows this full well.

Even the Buddha's own hands couldn't block the appear-
    ance of objects to the consciousness;
A great yogi knows there is no object behind the appear-
    ance.

"BUT DO SUCH experiences come about step by step?" asked the yogi.
"Or is it all at once?"

"Skilled individuals get it at once," answered Milarepa. "It comes
more gradually for those of average and mediocre abilities. Some
develop definitive realization, others don't, and others still get signs
that *look like* realization, but aren't really." And he sang the Song of
Distinguishing the Four Yogas:[15]

I bow down at the feet of the supreme Lama!

It's the mind fixated on objects that causes samsara.
If you recognize as spontaneous
The luminous self-awareness, free of fixation,
You'll taste the fruit of the first yoga, one-pointedness.

Some talk and talk about union, but their meditation is all
    conceptual,
They talk and talk about cause and effect, but their actions
    are flawed.
Such petty, deluded meditations
Have no place in the yoga of one-pointedness.

Luminous mind itself, free of fixation,
Is naturally blissful, without constructs.
If you recognize your very essence to be as clear as space,
You'll taste the fruit of the second yoga, simplicity.

Some talk and talk about no elaboration, but they elaborate
    plenty,
They talk and talk about the inexpressible, but they've got
    plenty of terminology.
Such self-obsessed meditations
Have no place in the yoga of simplicity.

In the dharma-body, appearance and emptiness are not two,
Samsara and nirvana are experienced as one.
If you know the Buddha and sentient beings to have the same
    identity,
As many have said, that's definitely the third yoga, one-taste.

Some talk and talk about oneness,
But they still want to make a point.
Such hazy confusion
Has no place in the yoga of one-taste.

Conceptual thoughts are by nature great awareness;
Cause and effect are non-dual, spontaneous.
They're the three-fold dimension of enlightenment,
And knowing this is the fruit of the fourth yoga, non-medi-
    tation.

Some talk and talk about non-meditation, but how active
    their mind is!
They talk and talk about clear light, but how confused their
    meditation is!
Such platitudes
Have no place in the yoga of non-meditation.

"Oh, what wonderful advice!" exclaimed the yogi from Kutang. "For us regular people, please give instructions on the six perfections!"[16] In response, Milarepa sang this song:

> At the feet of my genuine Lama, I bow down!
>
> Wealth and property are like dew on a grass blade,
> Give generously, don't be small-minded.
>
> This life you have is full of potential,
> Guard your ethics like your own eyes.
>
> Lower rebirths are the result of anger,
> Learn patience, even if it takes your whole life.
>
> If you're lazy, you won't benefit others,
> Be diligent in your good practice.
>
> If you're confused, you won't realize the essence of
>   Mahayana,[17]
> Meditate with a one-pointed mind on the ultimate meaning.
>
> You can search all you want, you won't find a Buddha,
> Look at the true nature of your own mind.
>
> Faith is like fog in the fall,
> If it dissipates, you must persevere.

The yogi, seized by an extraordinary feeling of devotion, returned home.

After a few days, a good many locals approached and placed offerings in front of the Jetsun. They showed him the highest respect, and arranged themselves around him. "We've been inspired by the story of your life," said one. "We wanted to meet you in person," said another. "We know you've gone through great austerities which have borne fruit in your practice. Tell us please how you developed your conviction," said a third. So the Jetsun sang the Song of the Six Convictions:

> When you dismiss worldly affairs,
> Strong faith will take root.
>
> It's hard to give up your homeland,
> But when you let go of patriotic feelings,
> Anger will dissolve.
>
> It's hard to deny the longing for friends,
> But when socializing stops,
> The needy mind will stop too.
>
> It's hard to stop wanting more stuff,
> But wear simple clothes,
> And your desires will be released.
>
> It's hard to say no to worldly lures,
> But keep a low profile,
> And your arrogance will deflate.
>
> It's hard not to be filled up with yourself.
> So all of you here today, patrons and faithful listeners,
> Go wander in the solitudes like an antelope!
> I've sung so far about conviction of perseverance.
>
> The dharma-body is just like the sky:
> It pervades you, it pervades all creatures,
> But due to pre-existing ignorance, you wander in samsara.
> You may get a glimpse of the real thing,
> But you have trouble stabilizing the experience.
> Without stability,
> Your mindstream sinks into the five poisons.

You're in the nebulous land of meaninglessness.
But when you gain meditative stability,
Your sensory consciousness arises but does not grasp.
You abide continuously in the three bodies.
That's conviction of realization.

Meditation and post-meditation are two separate things for
    beginners,
But when your mind is stable, you won't perceive them as
    separate.
In the yoga of non-distraction,
Your sensory consciousness arises but does not grasp.
You abide continuously in the three bodies,
You advance, unbound and energized,
You have wish-fulfilling powers.
If you're skilled, you meditate that all is like space
And have no attachment, whatever you do.
You recognize appearances as clouds
And don't fall for forms.
You think always of other beings
And you know these conventional forms to be like illusions.
You don't grasp—why grasp at the moon reflecting in the
    water?
Not grasping at things, you stay pure,
Just like the lotus that grows out of mud.
That's conviction of conduct.

Mind is like space in the sense that it's all-pervasive
It illuminates all situations as pure dharma-body
It's specific and demonstrative
Clear as a crystal in your hand.
At first, there's no coming
Then there's no staying
And in the end, there's no going.
Mind abides equally in past, present and future
Therefore mind is not born and does not die.

Like the sky, it is pure from time immemorial
And like cloud banks, the red and white elements dissolve
    of themselves.
Ultimately, you can't find a trace element of earth, water,
    fire or air.
As for this mind, it's pure and pervasive like space
It's inseparable from the unborn flux
But it cuts through the flow of samsara's realms.
That's conviction of one's practice blossoming.

Eventually you shed this illusory body,
And if you're realized, when you come to the in-between
    world—the bardo—
You perfect all qualities.
Guided by a profound ear-whispered instruction
Your mind is like a mother and her child reuniting.[18]
But if no such reunion happens,
This base illusory body
(Thanks to an instruction on spontaneous purity)
Still arises as pure enjoyment body.
If you understand the enjoyment body to be like a mirage
You never stray from the path.
That's conviction of the bardo of no delusion.

THIS SONG INSTILLED deep faith in the locals gathered around Milarepa. They left but then returned with further offerings and attentions.

AT DAWN ONE MORNING, the Jetsun experienced a state of illumination and heard Vajrayogini[19] prophesy, "Milarepa, you'll have a sun-disciple, a moon-disciple, and twenty-three star-disciples—that's twenty-five adepts in total. Also among your disciples will be one hundred with realizations, who won't regress; one hundred and eight who will generate the inner heat characteristic of the first stage; and one thousand and one of both sexes who will enter the path. Then there'll be all those who connect with you and will be spared lower rebirths forever, and those are too many to count. In Upper Gungtang is an individual with good karma, the one who will be like a moon. Go there for his sake!"

Milarepa resolved to go to Gungtang.

5

SONGS OF REALIZATION

Namo guru!

MILAREPA LEFT MANGYUL and arrived at Nyanang where his long-time patrons were euphoric to see him and begged him to stay for good. At the foot of a tree was a large boulder shaped like a belly with a cave in its underside: Belly Cave. That's where Milarepa settled and that's where, after a few days, the teacher Shakya Guna and several locals found him.

"Jetsun," they said, "you've traveled all over and stayed in many natural retreats. How was your practice? What convictions did you gain?" In response, Milarepa sang this Song of Gaining Confidence:

> At the feet of Marpa the translator, I bow down!
> Meditating in different mountain retreats:
>
> I gained confidence that there is no arising.
> Past and future lives are no longer two,
> Phantasms of the six realms[20] are no longer true,
> Distortions of birth and death have been all cut through.
>
> I gained confidence that all is equal.
> Pain and pleasure are no longer two,

Emotional games are no longer true,
Saying "yes" to this, "no" to that, has been all cut through.

I gained confidence that there's no separation.
Samsara and nirvana are no longer two,
Stages and paths are no longer true,
Hopes and fears have been all cut through.

THE LOCALS NOW asked Milarepa about his different experiences. "My friends, to please you I'll sing a Song of Experience," he said and sang:

Externally, the circumstances were set up: my mother and
    father.
Internally, the basic consciousness came up.
In between, I got this fine human body.
I just avoided birth in the lower realms.

Externally, birth and death seemed to take place.
Internally, faith and renunciation came up.
In between, I remembered the holy dharma.
I just didn't make enemies.

Externally, the condition was set up: my Lama.
Internally, the awareness shone from my studies.
In between, I gained certainty.
I just didn't doubt the dharma.

Externally, the six kinds of beings appeared.
Internally, non-referential compassion came up.
In between, I stayed mindful of my meditation experience.
I just didn't let my compassion get all gooey.

Externally, the three realms shone, naturally liberated.
Internally, great awareness came up spontaneously.

In between, I gained confidence in my realizations.
I just stayed on the ultimate truth without fear.

Externally, all kinds of sensual pleasures arose.
Internally, the wisdom of no grasping came up.
In between, I developed the practice of one taste.
I just didn't take pain and pleasure as two.

Externally, there was building up and breaking down.
Internally, freedom from hopes and fears came up.
In between, I stayed clear of designs.
I just didn't make a split between good and evil.

THE TEACHER SHAKYA GUNA spoke up, "Jetsun, your practice has always been extraordinary. I've been with you before, but I never got a definitive instruction. Please give me instructions and empowerments, be kind to me, it would help set my mind straight!" The Jetsun did so and then sent him to meditate.

Soon Shakya Guna returned to Milarepa with questions about his experiences, "If samsara and nirvana don't exist, why practice? If there's no mind, how will I ever become a scholar? If there's no Lama, who's there to teach me how to practice? Please clear this up and point out the nature of mind!"

Milarepa answered with a Song on the Nature of Mind:

By nature appearances do not arise.
If they seem to arise, you're clinging to things as real.

By nature samsara is groundless.
If it seems to have ground, you're stuck in conceptual
    thought.

By nature mind is unified.
If it seems to have distinct features, you're caught in grasping.

By nature the Lama holds the transmission.
If you make things up yourself, you're deluded.

Think of mind as the sky:
Conceptual thoughts, like clouds, obscure it,
But an oral instruction from a genuine Lama
Will blow away the clouds.

Conceptual thoughts themselves are in fact clear light,
And experiences shine like the sun or the moon,
Beyond time, beyond mandate,[21]
Beyond reference points, beyond words.

Truths are bright as stars.
What dawns is great bliss,
Natural, genuine dharma-body,
Empty of consciousness' conditioning.[22]

Abide in the flow of wisdom free of fixation:
It's a spontaneous occurrence, pure and effortless,
Intrinsically relaxed,
All dimensions as one. How marvelous!

"TEACHER," CONTINUED MILAREPA after he had finished singing, "don't get hung up on fame or pleasures. Don't go for the superficial words. Practice your whole life." And the Jetsun burst into this Song on the Importance of Practice:

Fortunate students gathered here,
Is this life insidious, or what?
Is your comfort an illusion, or not?
And your happiness—a bit like a dream, maybe?
Now praised, now criticized—just an echo, or something more?
Is what appears the same as mind—is it?
Isn't your mind in fact the Buddha?

And the Buddha, dharma-body?
And dharma-body, reality itself?
If you get my meaning, you'll understand that all appear-
    ances are referenced in mind.
Look at your mind day and night:
You're looking but you can't see it.
Rest in the non-seeing then.

I *am* Mahamudra,[23]
There's no higher, other nature.
I let my awareness settle without fixation.
Because there's no difference between meditation and post-
    meditation,
I don't get into "levels" of meditation.
Because whatever appears is empty of self-nature,
I stay mindful and do neither apprehension nor non-appre-
    hension.
I've tasted the flavor of no arising,
I've meditated on thatness,
And these are superior to all the others—
Superior to tantric *karmamudra*,[24]
To practices with the energies, channels and seed essence
    of the body,
To mantra recitation and deity visualization,
To meditations on love, compassion, joy or equanimity,
All of which are mere introductions to the great vehicle
And do not wipe out anger and attachment.
Understand that all appearances are not different from mind
And that mind itself is empty.
 If you stay with this experience, this realization,
You'll complete your practices, ethics and all.

THE TEACHER SHAKYA GUNA practiced accordingly and gave birth to
extraordinary realizations. He became a close son-disciple of Milarepa.

6

SONGS AT THE INN

Namo guru!

THE JETSUN MILAREPA meditated at North Horse for a while, then moved on towards Shriri. He made a stop at the Yeru Gang Inn on the way. The inn was crowded: Doctor Yaru Tankpa was there with his whole retinue of monks, as well as the merchant Dawa Norbu and his crowd.

When Milarepa approached the merchants to ask for alms, Dawa Norbu gave him a black look. "You yogis are all the same! You lead the good life on the backs of others, why don't you make your own money? Better for everyone if you did."

Milarepa replied, "Oh, you're so pleased with yourself the way you live. But somehow you've missed the part where your happiness today is your misery tomorrow. Listen well, I've got a song for you about Things to Keep in Mind." And he sang:

> You love mansions and exclusive neighborhoods,
> But when you die, you're down and out.
> It doesn't hurt to keep this in mind.
>
> You love puffing your chest and talking big,
> But when you die, you're on your own.
> It doesn't hurt to keep this in mind.

You love your friends and your family
But when you die, you leave your children.
It doesn't hurt to keep this in mind.

You love your people and your wealth,
But when you die, you go empty-handed.
It doesn't hurt to keep this in mind.

You love your strength and your skill,
But when you die, your body's just a corpse.
It doesn't hurt to keep this in mind.

You love your sharp, quick senses,
But when you die, your mind goes soft.
It doesn't hurt to keep this in mind.

You love good flavors and fine food,
But when you're dying, you're lucky if you can get water
    down.
It doesn't hurt to keep this in mind.

Thinking of this makes me practice dharma.
I don't care for your secular pleasures, I'm happy!

At Yeru Gang Inn,
I, the yogi Milarepa, sing this song
Of Things to Keep in Mind.
May it inspire you to practice virtue!

THE SONG HAD a strong effect on Dawa Norbu. With deep emotion, the merchant said, "You've really got it right, Lama. I'm even thinking about the dharma now! Can you please give me an oral instruction that I can put to practice?"

In response, Milarepa sang a Song of Oral Instructions:

Natural retreats are quality places.
The Lama who sees and acts is a quality gem,
Pray to him with sincere faith
And practice correctly.

If your mind is agitated, use the view:
Mental labels will peel off on their own.
Quite marvelous, really!

If your mind is hard, ask for alms:
Solid objects will dissolve on their own.
Quite marvelous, really!

You dislike meditation?
Discuss it with others of experience,
The comparison will help your mind.

You have doubts?
Look at the words of the Buddha,
Their truth will give you conviction.

Feeling unhappy?
Pray to the Lama,
His or her blessings will ease your mind.

Observe self-indulgent men
Watch them lie in samsara's bed
Watch their heads sink into the five poisons:
Greed, hatred, pride, ignorance and envy
Watch them spit their afflictions to the winds.
Find these men a doctor!
Diagnose them through devotion of body, speech and mind
As medicine, apply the pointing-out instructions
Of the Lama's six qualities.
No doubt they'll recover from the poisons.
Then, make offerings in gratitude.

THE MERCHANT WAS completely overcome with devotion. Though he stayed a layman, still he practiced well and over time he became an excellent yogi.

BUT LET'S TURN to Doctor Yaru Tankpa, mentioned briefly at the beginning of this story. While Milarepa was at the inn, begging in his usual fashion, Doctor Yaru was expounding on the dharma. His students were used to spending their evenings in prayer and meditation, their days in practice.

One day, Milarepa approached them at lunch, asking for food. More than a few spoke their minds at the sight, "Would you look at this yogi!" "He seems out of his depth. Doesn't study, doesn't practice!" "Probably incapable of entering into deep meditation." "I bet he can't recite a single mantra." "I feel sorry for him!" "Now he's down to begging from the monks."

"I do it all at once," replied Milarepa. "I meditate on the deity and I recite mantras, and I study and practice, and I enter into deep meditation. All at once. I'm happy. Now here's a song for you." And he sang the Song of Good Yoga:

> Buddha, dharma, sangha, the three gems,
> Give all the support.
> In non-fabricated awareness, I've perfected them.
> Why would I pray to them?
> No mantras, no prayers: that's good yoga!

> Yidam deities lead to attainments
> Common and extraordinary.
> In non-visualized clear light, I've fine-tuned them.
> Why would I practice the generation stage?
> One's body as deity-body: that's good yoga!

> Dakinis sweep away obstacles
> And dispel misery.
> In the natural state, I've realized this.

Why would I make *torma* offerings?[25]
Sense consciousness and sense objects at ease: that's good
  yoga!

Conceptual thinking is a hellish trick,
A demonic display.
In the state of reality, I've worked it out.
Why would I perform exorcisms?
Conceptual thinking shining as dharma-body: that's good
  yoga!

Mainstream texts and essays
Are so much logic.
In luminous experience, I've absorbed them all.
Why would I study?
Appearances read as a book: that's good yoga!

DOCTOR YARU'S VOICE was heard, "Yogi, your practice seems extraordinary. But the Buddhist teachings are quite clear: you should study,
especially in the beginning. It's also recommended that people follow the monastic route, and that they practice virtue."

To this Milarepa said, "That's your way, I've got no problems with
that. Myself, I do it Milarepa's way, which is shameless. Whereas—
correct me if I'm wrong, doctor—I've got a feeling your style is a bit
like this—" and he sang the Song to a Doctor:

I take refuge in the three jewels.
Lama, hold me in your compassionate heart!
Doctor, specialist of the mundane,
If you haven't trained your own mind within,
How do you expect to train the wild minds of beings?

What a lovely peacock by that white umbrella—
But oh! It's flitted away, quick as lightning.
Am I right, doctor?

That monastery kitchen behind the town,
What a den of thieves, what duplicity!
Am I right, doctor?

Wild pandemonium, crazed parties,
Feels like everyone around you is the enemy.
Am I right, doctor?

Caring for horses, sheep and assets
Seems like small flowers in the face of a gale.
Am I right, doctor?

The body, swollen with passions
Is like a corpse, doused and swathed.
Am I right, doctor?

A woman who dares to practice
Is a shameful stain on any tradition.
Am I right, doctor?

So much good food for religious offerings—
Feels like having to pay taxes.
Am I right, doctor?

Divination, animism, astrology:
It's the work of the devil!
Am I right, doctor?

This small song sticks in your head,
Oh, evil, evil thoughts!
Am I right, doctor?

Country, property, ownership:
That's a con-game, a racket, a rainbow.
Don't you think so?

Brainwashing disciples by deception:
That's working for too many masters.
Don't you think so?

Teaching the dharma without knowing its truth:
That's playing with people's heads.
Don't you think so?

Very, very hard to help others
If you can't help yourself!

THE SONG SPARKED an immense respect in Doctor Yaru Tankpa. He got off his seat, approached Milarepa and bowed down. As tears washed down his face, he said, "How true, how true to the dharma."

One of Doctor Yaru's students, Seben Tönchung, attached himself to Milarepa. He was given empowerments and oral instructions, and attained high realizations. He will reappear in later stories as Seben Repa.

7

My walking stick

Namo guru!

THE PLAN WAS simple enough: Jetsun Milarepa and his disciple Seben
Repa would go to Chenlung Valley and beg for alms. As they marched,
Milarepa leaned on his walking stick—the only thing to his name.
Milarepa had long given up on possessions.

On the way, they reached a house that was nailed shut. No one
there except an old crone. When Milarepa asked her to spare some
food, she crackled back, "I'm poor, I've got nothing! Go back across
the fields, you'll find a landowner named Dzong. Rich man. He'll
give you what you want, just ask him."

The Jetsun and his son-disciple Seben Repa found the man in his
grain store, arranging his different seeds.

"Patron!" said Milarepa, "We're told you're rich. We're yogis and
we've come a long way, we're begging for food."

"Always glad to oblige!" replied the landowner. "You're yogis, then?
Use my cattle as an example and sing me something to do with farming."

Milarepa and Seben Repa sang together this Song about Farming :

> Well then, arrogant patron,
> Listen here, rich man!

For three months in the spring,
Tibetan farmers plough their fields.

We, the yogis, sow our fields as well:
The hard ground of neurotic emotions
Is fertilized with preliminary practices
And moistened with the five nectars.
There, with a noble, knowing mind,
We plant the seed of non-confusion and non-conceptuality.
Then, we harvest the fields with the oxen of non-duality,
Which is harnessed with wisdom
Whipped by the samaya commitment
Led by non-distraction
And spurred by diligence.
Such methods
Help bodhichitta sprout
And eventually bear fruit.

You're good with worldly farming,
We're more into ultimate farming.
At harvest, you look again and again at your crop,
But in the long run, who is happiest?

This was an allegorical song,
Using farming as an example.
Be happy, proud man!
If you take in this meaning, you'll create much merit.

THE LANDOWNER DZONG responded by pointing to Milarepa's walking stick, "Yogi, I'm curious—this thing in your hand, is it a toy for kids, or for loonies, or what?"

In reply, Milarepa sang the Song of the White Walking Stick:

Well then, inquisitive patron,
Listen here, charitable soul!

Do you know who I am?
In case you don't—
I'm Milarepa.
I'm an ascetic
A hardy meditator
A yogi without bias.

This walking stick you see in my hand
First grew out of a boulder
It was cut with a sickle
Then smoothed with leather
It comes from Mön in the south
I've attached loads of Mahayana texts to it
And traveled many markets with it
Well, that's my walking stick.

Do you get what I'm saying?
If you don't,
Listen carefully, I will spell it all out.

The stout end of the stick, cut from the tree root
Is a symbol of cutting samsara at the root.
The fine end of the stick, cut at the top of the tree
Represents the cutting of doubt and deviation.
Its two-foot length
Suggests the two accumulations.[26]
Its quality and pliancy
Signal the excellence of original mind itself.
The delicate varnish
Hints at the refinement of mind's naked state.
It is both straight and flexible,
A symbol for the correct way to practice.
The grooves on the stick
Represent the perfection of bodhichitta.
Its four sections
Indicate the four immeasurables.[27]

The stick has three knots,
Just as we speak of three bodies in the basic state.
It doesn't change color,
Conveying the unchanging basis of reality itself.
Its top is round,
A sign for reality free of fabrication.
Its original white shine
Represents the stainless nature of the dharma-body.
The stick is hollow at the core,
Just as all phenomena are empty of true nature.
It has a speckle,
A symbol for the knowing of the single sphere.
There are darker stains on the stick,
Suggesting the continued presence of subtle concepts
In the minds of Tibetan yogis.
This stick has been good from the first day,
As is practice in accord with the dharma.
It's appealing and agreeable,
A symbol for the attractiveness of faithful beings.
Its base, carved from iron,
Conveys the yogi's endurance in solitary practice.
Its handle, plated with copper,
Indicates the force of dakinis gathered.
The nail hammered to the tip
Is a sign for a yogi's perseverance.
Its brass ring
Represents the development of inner qualities.
It's smoothed with leather,
Showing a yogi's pliant wisdom.
It has two plaited straps,
Symbolizing union on the path.
The larger and smaller straps joining together
Conveys the meeting of the three bodies with the mother
    wisdom.
Bone ornaments hanging on the stick
Represent many travels for a yogi.

The tinder-pouch of flint
Is a sign to take all appearances as friends.
The white conch shell attached to the side
Indicates the turning of the dharma wheel.
The rag made with the skin of a wild beast
Suggests absence of fear or anxiety.
The little mirror here
Shows realizations dawning within.
The sharp knife
Hints at the slicing of afflictive emotions.
The hanging crystal
Conveys the purification of habitual patterns.
The ivory rosary is linked to the stick
Just as the mind is connected to the Lama.
The ringing bells
Represent my widespread fame.
The cotton cords in red and white
Signal a great circle of disciples.

This beautiful stick that I hold here
Symbolizes victory over darkness.
Your curiosity about my walking stick
Shows a tendency for devotion.
Our meeting here today
Indicates good merit gathered in the past.
I've sung this Song of the White Walking Stick,
A song of symbols, signs and metaphors.
May you be inspired and understand its meaning.
May you be happy always and practice the holy dharma!

THIS WAS MILAREPA'S song, in accord with the dharma. It had its effect on Dzong, who prostrated and placed his head at Milarepa's feet with heartfelt respect.

"Lama!" he said. "I'll be your patron to the day I die. Please accept my hospitality, be my guest here." The Jetsun and his disciple Seben

Repa stayed for a full week, but would not stay a day beyond that. As Milarepa explained, "We're not after your worldly offerings."

So the patron Dzong said, "If you must go, please give me a few words about meditative experience." In response, Milarepa and Seben Repa sang together a Song about Meditative Experience :

> Well then, inspired patron,
> Listen here, rich, careless man!
> Dharma words are easy,
> Dharma practice is hard.
>
> You're a man of the world, and a confused one at that.
> You're wasting your spare hours:
> "I'll do dharma," you say, but life is going by.
> Well, *now* is the time to practice.
>
> Mountain spring water is cool, wholesome,
> Full of medicinal properties—
> Beneficial for the grouse and the mountain birds,
> But out of reach of the animals below.
>
> A thunderbolt, like a mighty sword,
> Can turn a battle around—
> Useful for the magical Earth Protector elephants,
> Not for the other, smaller elephants.
>
> The heavenly nectar of immortality
> Replenishes the body—
> Good for the great Nagarjuna,
> But no help for normal practitioners.
>
> The gold dripping from death's demonic spirits
> Is enough to remove all poverty—
> Good for the Prince of Moonlight,
> But not so for the common people.

Deep in the ocean, the wish-fulfilling gem
Can answer all desires—
Useful for Takshaka, the serpent king of mythology,
But not for the people of this world.

The palace of the Joyous Heaven
Offers an incredible view—
Good for the great Asanga,
But not for the eyes of ordinary beings.

The six medicinal plants[28]
Clear problems of heat and cold—
Good when they're made right,
But not otherwise.

In terms of cause and effect, the ten virtues
Result in a higher rebirth—
Powerful for those who believe,
But not for sinners out of control.

The Lama's oral instructions
Lead to enlightenment—
Good for those with good karma,
But no help for the less fortunate.

The precious ear-whispered teaching
Takes you to Buddhahood without doubt—
Essential for practitioners who persist,
But not for lazy meditators—and that includes you.

Food and drink, a meal, a feast
Eliminate hunger and poverty—
Enjoyable for some,
But not for the greedy.
Generosity, magnanimity:
These are about providing—

Something you have shown, patron Dzong,
But few rich men are like you.

I, the yogi Milarepa,
And I, the student Seben Repa,
And you, the patron Dzong,
Have spent seven days together.
Our meeting is the fruit of previous merit.
We're going now, we won't stay.
May you and those around you
Enjoy good health and a long life!

"SEE, YOU GAVE me food, you gave me shelter, and I gave you dharma," added Milarepa. "We made an exchange, and it created an important relationship between us. As a farmer, you know seeds, and now the seed of dharma has been planted in you. The fruit is the wisdom that blooms spontaneously at every moment.

"Actually," continued the Jetsun, "you need sincere aspiration, but beyond that, you don't need too many dharma teachings. You don't need to wander from place to place. You don't need to be around Lamas all the time—anyway, intimacy breeds contempt. If you're devoted and lucky, then even if you go off for a while, the power of your aspiration will set you right again. That's why a devoted and aspiring mind is so crucial. These days, people don't gather much merit; as a result, they fail to see inner qualities, yet they have no problems pointing to external failings, no matter how small. But those who only see faults in others are usually ignorant themselves. Mostly, you should look at your mental patterns. Practice well now, it will pay off in the future.

"Locals here don't practice much," concluded Milarepa. "They like to think that there's no place as beautiful as their homeland, and they love big celebrations. But watch out for the narrow mind. Fact is, if you always give to beggars, that's enough. A fox can't jump where the lion leaps: he'd only break a limb. Most practitioners can't practice the way I do. May you keep the faith, rich man Dzong."

AND WITH THIS, Milarepa and Seben Repa left to beg for alms. In a town, they met a tantric teacher who asked, "Where do you yogis come from? Do you have pure view, meditation and conduct? You look like you just might. What can you tell me that would enhance my practice?"

So the Jetsun Milarepa replied, "Do *you* understand pure view, meditation and conduct? I could tell you about mine if you don't. But perhaps you should give us alms to establish a good karmic link."

"Sure, giving you alms is a good idea. I thought you'd like to know that being a tantric teacher, I know something about view, meditation and conduct." And he gave a very long explanation of view, meditation and conduct based on the system he followed. He concluded, "What do you say?"

The Jetsun Milarepa responded, "Maybe you're terrified of samsara's cycle and you want out. Maybe you practice undistracted on the Lama's instructions. Maybe you're really determined to attain enlightenment quickly. But then again, maybe you're just spouting words, words, words." And he sang this Song about Going Down the Wrong Track :

> Oh, do listen, you grand teacher!
> How can you benefit others
> When your mind won't let go of this life?
> If you don't realize samsara and nirvana as one,
> Mistaking coarse, common experience
> For the unsurpassed practice of one taste,
> Aren't you carried off by the torrents of the eight worldly
>   concerns?[29]
>
> Do you realize the non-dual view free of extremes
> Or are you caught in a tetralemma?[30]
>
> Failing to put your mind to meditation,
> Are you bound by labels?

And your meditative great bliss,
Is that anything but a deluded state of desire?

Are you caught in a practice
That lacks blessings of body and speech?

When you meditate on appearances as the Lama,
Is your awareness failing?

You teach through tantric symbols,
But do you teach that symbols have no truth?

Your own mind is pure from the beginning,
Are you spoiling it with lies and fictions?

In your actions, are you doing
What a good Lama would never do?

You want to get further in this life,
But aren't these the greatest of obstacles?

If you're not practicing the view and meditation
Of a lineage with blessings,
You're the dupe of demons,
And you won't free yourself from lower rebirths.
That's why you must rely on a pure lineage, a pure trans-
    mission,
And practice without self-interest.

THE TANTRIC TEACHER was stirred by this song. "Now that's wonderful!" he exclaimed with deep faith. He prostrated, placed Milarepa's
feet on his head, and invited him into his own house, where he showed
the greatest hospitality. He even asked Milarepa to take him along as
an attendant. The Jetsun recognized him as a person of good karma

and accepted. They left for Lashi, where Milarepa granted the teacher maturing and liberating empowerments and instructions. The teacher became a heart-disciple of Milarepa and was later famous as Teacher Jangchub Gyal.

This was the story of Milarepa's walking stick and his meeting with the tantric teacher Jangchub Gyal.

8

White Rock Vajra Fortress Cave

Namo guru!

Milarepa and his disciples circumambulated Mount Kailash[31] and then returned to White Rock Vajra Fortress Cave. Patrons of old came to enquire about his health. Milarepa assured them he was well, and in turn they said with feeling that thanks to his blessings, things had been going well, no recent loss or recent death to relate. Mostly they were happy he was back and asked about his visit to Mount Kailash, and what delights that had brought.

So the Jetsun sang the Song of Twelve Yogic Delights:

> Like escaping from the abyss of dark deeds,
> Happy is the yoga of abandoning one's fatherland.
>
> Like a horse freeing itself from its bridle,
> Happy is the yoga free of perceiver and perceived.
>
> Like a wounded antelope staying put,
> Happy is the yoga of living in solitude.
>
> Like the king of birds soaring in the sky,
> Happy is the yoga of gaining certainty in the view.

Like the vulture flying higher and higher,
Happy is the yoga of no obstruction.

Like the shepherd caring for his flock of sheep,
Happy is the yoga of protecting the experience of clear light
    and emptiness.

Like stable Mount Meru,
Happy is unchanging yoga.

Like the flow of great rivers,
Happy is the yoga of continuous experience.

Like a human corpse in a charnel ground,
Happy is yoga without action.

Like throwing a rock into the ocean,
Happy is the yoga of no returning.

Like the sun shining in the sky,
Happy is all-illuminating yoga.

Like the falling leaves of a palm-tree,
Happy is the yoga of no rebirth.

This is my song of twelve yogic delights,
A little dharma offered in response to your request, patrons.

THIS SONG INSPIRED the group of patrons who said goodbye and returned home.

AT THAT POINT, to gauge the extent of Rechungpa's renunciation of
samsara, his experience and his realization, Milarepa sang him the
Song of Twelve Deceptions:

Since worldly affairs are so deceptive,
I pursue the true meaning.

Since distractions and busyness are so deceptive,
I practice non-duality.

Since entourage and servants are so deceptive,
I wander alone in charnel grounds.

Since wealth and possessions are so deceptive,
I give whatever I have.

Since external appearances are so deceptive,
I look at the mind within.

Since conceptual thoughts are so deceptive,
I follow primordial awareness.

Since conventional truths are so deceptive,
I ascertain the ultimate truth.

Since scribbles and books are so deceptive,
I meditate on the ear-whispered instructions.

Since technical explanations are so deceptive,
I rest naturally, without contrivance.

Since the cycle of birth and death is so deceptive,
I look at the birthless truth.

Since ordinary knowledge is so deceptive,
I practice the natural play of awareness.

Since exercises of "Fixing the Mind" are so deceptive,
I relax in the natural state.

AT THIS, RECHUNGPA thought, *My Lama is really the Buddha. His dharma is the real thing. He obviously sang this for those who, like myself, lack devotion.* So in reply, Rechungpa offered a song about his own experience of view, meditation and conduct.

> Father Lama, Jetsun, please listen to me!
> My afflicted mind is full of darkness.
> I supplicate you: please hold me with the lasso of your compassion!
>
> At the crossroad of eternalism and nihilism,
> I've gone astray from the view free of extremes.
> I haven't arrived at a conclusion about the natural state.
>
> At the crossroad of dullness and agitation,
> I've lost my way from meditation on emptiness-clear-light inseparable.
> I lack the will to reverse attachment.
>
> At the crossroad of taking up and abandoning,
> I've lost my way from spontaneous conduct.
> I don't really want my delusions to end!
>
> At the crossroad of fraud and pretense,
> I've failed to keep pure my samaya vow.
> I haven't conquered deceit—or hypocrisy.
>
> At the crossroad of samsara and nirvana,
> I've moved away from my mind being the Buddha.
> I'm not ready for dharma-body realizations!
>
> At the crossroad of hope and fear,
> I've gone astray from the fruit: the four dimensions of enlightenment.
> I still don't know my own face.

Dear father Lama
You've taken care of me with great kindness.
Please protect me now and in the future!

IN RESPONSE, JETSUN MILAREPA said, "Rechungpa, those are not the experiences and realizations you've had! Don't pretend you know nothing. Be honest about it." And because of Milarepa's compassion, Rechungpa underwent a sudden leap in his experiences and realizations. He offered this Song of Treasures:

It is through the kindness of my father Lama
That I have realized these treasures.

I found emptiness within appearances.
Now I no longer think that things actually exist.

I found dharma-body within emptiness.
Now I no longer think of begging for alms.

I found non-duality within multiplicity.
Now I no longer think of meeting and separation.

I found sameness within red and white.
Now I no longer think there is such a thing as "pure" practice.

JETSUN REPLIED, "RECHUNGPA, your meditation experience is nearly there, but not quite. Real meditation experience is like this—" And he sang the Song of Eight Perfect Understandings:

If appearance and emptiness are inseparable,
That's mastery of the view.

If daily life and dreams at night are inseparable,
That's mastery of meditation.

If bliss and emptiness are inseparable,
That's mastery of conduct.

If this life and other lives are inseparable,
That's mastery of the natural state.

If there's no distinction between mind and space,
That's mastery of the dharma-body.

If there's no distinction between joy and sorrow,
That's mastery of the oral instructions.

If there's no distinction between afflictive emotions and primordial awareness,
That's ultimate realization.

If there's no distinction between one's own mind and the Buddha,
That's fruition realized.

RECHUNGPA'S REALIZATIONS gradually developed, thanks to Milarepa. To show the understanding he had gained through practice, Rechungpa sang the Song of the Six Bardos, or the Six In-Between States:

To all the lord-Lamas, I bow down!
In the bardo of appearance and emptiness,
There is no object of eternalism or nihilism.
I don't stick to conceptual tenets.
Now I'm beyond birth, beyond labels.
That's the view of this alms-seeker.
I won't be shamed in a circle of realized beings.

In the bardo of bliss and emptiness,
There is no object to focus on.

I don't do mental fixations.
Now I rest in the naked state, free of distractions.
That's the meditation of this alms-seeker.
I won't be shamed in a circle of experienced sages.

In the bardo of attachment and non-attachment,
There is no object that can offer happiness.
I say no to a life of deceit.
Now whatever appears is my friend.
That's the conduct of this alms-seeker.
I won't be shamed in a circle of accomplished yogis.

In the bardo of faulty and faultless,
There is no pure or impure.
I don't do fraud.
Now my own mind is my witness.
That's the samaya of this alms-seeker.
I won't be shamed in a circle of disciplined friends.

In the bardo of samsara and nirvana,
There are no Buddhas and no sentient beings.
I'm not hanging on hopes and fears.
Now suffering arises as bliss.
That's the fruition of this alms-seeker.
I won't be shamed in a circle of adepts.

In the bardo of words and meaning,
There's no place for scholars of the conventional.
I don't have doubt or hesitation.
Now samsaric appearances arise as dharma-body.
That's the realization of this alms-seeker.
I won't be shamed in a circle of the wise.

MILAREPA WAS DELIGHTED with Rechungpa's song, "This is real experience! You are a worthy vessel, as they say. At first, you made me

happy with your faith and knowledge. Later, you listened, reflected
and engaged in tantric Mahayana.³² You practiced and persevered in
your meditation. In the end, you gradually developed superior realization. Myself, I don't care for talkative students. In order to practice, you must be introspective and meditate. I'm going to tell you
what my Lama, Marpa, said to me, 'It's fine to have not much knowledge of the sutras and tantras. Don't go after conventional terminol-
ogy. Look within and meditate just as the Lama says. Remember the
Lama's words, and practice. You will surely turn away from samsara,
and all qualities will blossom in your mindstream.' Now I've passed
my Lama's words to you!"

Rechungpa asked what else Marpa had said, so the Jetsun sang the
Song of My Lama's Sayings:

> The three gems are the best support,
> Steady faith is the best of friends,
> Conceptual thought, the worst demon,
> Pride, the vilest evil,
> Denial, the greatest sin,
> Jealousy, the most harmful path.
>
> If you don't cleanse your dark deeds with the four opponent
>   powers,³³
> You'll wander among the beings of the six realms.
>
> If you don't make an effort to accumulate merit,
> You won't attain the bliss of liberation.
>
> If you don't give up the ten evil deeds,
> You'll experience the suffering of the lower realms.
>
> If you don't meditate on emptiness and compassion,
> You won't reach ultimate enlightenment.
>
> If you want to attain Buddhahood in this very life,
> Look undistracted at the mind.

Meditate on the Six Yogas[34]—
The essential meaning of the tantras.

Meditate on mantra techniques—
The essential meaning of the oral instructions.

If you go after wealth, honor, or fame,
You're heading straight into the mouth of Mara, Lord of
    Death.

If you praise yourself while belittling others,
You'll fall into a samsaric abyss.

If you don't tame the elephant of mind,
You'll miss the point of the oral instructions.

The greatest merit is to arouse bodhichitta.
The view beyond birth is best.
Practice is the most profound path.
Really practice with the channels and seed essence.
Behold the co-emergent face.
Rely on a holy master.
Don't waste your life with pettiness.
Look at your own unborn mind.
Don't expect happiness in samsara.
Don't think negatively of suffering.
Realize your own mind, and you'll be a Buddha.
There's no need to talk much,
These words say it all.
Integrate them in your experience!

RECHUNGPA TOOK THIS to heart and his realization improved.

NEXT, MILAREPA AND HIS disciples settled to do ascetic practice. A
host of dakinis surrounded them and said to the Jetsun, "Milarepa,

when you practice view, meditation and conduct, you'll find that your realizations improve if you accept a little human food and a little dakini sustenance. We're here to provide for you." The Jetsun replied, "How could wealth, food and enjoyments be any more marvelous than the qualities gained in mental realization?" And he sang the Song of the Suitable:

> To all father Lamas, I bow down!
>
> I, the yogi Milarepa,
> Sing a song in the natural state.
>
> Mother dakinis gathered here,
> Dancing in the realm of non-existence: listen!
>
> Conviction of cause and effect
> Isn't equaled by ordinary faith.
>
> Living alone in solitude
> Isn't equaled by ordinary samadhi.
>
> This meditative equipoise beyond subject and object
> Isn't equaled by ordinary view.
>
> This unforgettable post-meditation
> Isn't equaled by ordinary practice.
>
> This mindfulness beyond words
> Isn't equaled by ordinary conduct.
>
> This union of emptiness and compassion
> Isn't equaled by ordinary results.
>
> This piece of cotton that always keeps me warm
> Isn't equaled by ordinary clothes.

This samadhi that knows no hunger
Isn't equaled by ordinary meat.

This nectar stream of bodhichitta
Isn't equaled by ordinary drink.

This contentment that arises within
Isn't equaled by ordinary food and wealth.

The translator Marpa Lotsawa
Isn't equaled by ordinary adepts.

Seeing the face of the deity—one's own mind—
Isn't equaled by ordinary yidam deities.

The yogi Milarepa
Isn't equaled by ordinary meditators.

This body free of illness
Isn't equaled by ordinary medicine.

Hosts of dakinis, listen!
Even where there is no light, light exists:
This luminosity is light.

Even where there is no heat, heat exists:
This cotton cloth is heat.

Even where there is no bliss, bliss exists:
This illusory body is bliss.

Even where there is no joy, joy exists:
This dream is joy.

I, the yogi, feel happy.
Is this White Rock Vajra Cave high or not high?

If White Rock Vajra Cave wasn't high,
How could vultures soar beneath it?

If the winds of the new year weren't icy,
How could the mountain streams freeze?

If *tummo* practice didn't heat me,
How could this Nepali cotton keep me warm?

If the food of samadhi didn't sustain me,
How could I have no hunger?

If I didn't drink of the bodhichitta stream,
How could I do without water?

If the Lama's oral instructions weren't profound,
How could I be free of demons?

If this yogi wasn't realized,
How could he wander in such a no-man's land?

All this is but the kindness of the Lama,
So let's practice!

THE DAKINIS SAID, "So it is! How marvelous! Tomorrow, a disciple with good karma will arrive. Take care of him!" And they disappeared like a rainbow.

AT THAT TIME, a few patrons from Kutang approached the Jetsun and his disciples with a request for dharma. Milarepa gave them the transmission for taking refuge and told them about the benefits of practice. One of the patrons now asked, "Do you also practice this 'taking refuge'?" The Jetsun replied, "Yes, it protects me completely, so I rely on it. You all should take such refuge in the Lama and the three jewels, and don't just mouth the words. I've told you already about

the benefits of practice, and now I'll sing a song to inspire you." And
he sang the Song of Refuge:

> To all lord-Lamas, I bow down!
>
> Buddha, dharma and sangha:
> These three are the outer sources of refuge.
> Even I take refuge in them.
> You should do the same.
>
> Lama, yidam and dakini:
> These three are the inner sources of refuge.
> Even I take refuge in them.
> You should do the same.
>
> Channels, energy flow and seed essence:
> These three are the secret sources of refuge.
> Even I take refuge in them.
> You should do the same.
>
> Appearance, emptiness and their inseparability:
> These three are the real sources of refuge.
> Even I take refuge in them.
> You should do the same.
>
> What shelter can there be from never-ending suffering
> If you don't take refuge?
>
> The storeroom of your illusory body
> Rots under the dripping rain day after day.
>
> The rotting storeroom of your illusory body
> Is sure to be destroyed.
>
> Look at the life path of the yogi Milarepa,
> Empty of intrinsic nature:

I'm a cluster that will fall apart at death.
It's just like the shadow of the setting sun:
Even as you try to run from it,
It gets closer and closer.

A dharma practitioner who looks at death
Learns about the value of virtue.
Again and again, the question arises,
Is there any joy?

A sinner who looks at death
Learns about good and evil.
Again and again the question arises,
Are there no regrets?

A rich man who looks at death
Learns that money is the enemy.
Again and again the question arises,
Can I let go of it all?

An old man who looks at death
Learns about impermanence.
Again and again the question arises,
Do I not feel disgusted at samsara?

A youngster who looks at death
Learns there's no free time in life.
Again and again the question arises,
Have I exerted myself in practice?

You like your parents to be happy
But what of the suffering they endure?

You like a fine fur coat,
But what if you don't have one?

Harvests eradicate poverty,
But what if you can't work?

You like a swift horse,
But what if you don't ride?

The dharma practitioner travels towards happiness,
But what of those who can't practice dharma?

To diminish your hunger,
Learn to give away.

To diminish your drowsiness,
Practice well!

Reflect on the suffering of the lower realms,
Practice, all of you!

THE PATRONS would return many more times to hear the dharma. One young man in particular, Ronchung Repa, developed unalterable faith in the Jetsun. He begged to follow as an attendant, and the Jetsun thought to himself, *This must be the one prophesied by the dakinis yesterday. I'd better take care of him.* He gave him teachings, empowerments, and oral instructions. Ronchung Repa attained maturation and liberation and became one of Milarepa's close disciples.

9

WHAT'S A KING?

Namo guru!

JETSUN MILAREPA WAS in silent retreat at Katya Cave in the mountains of Mön when a group of local hunters stumbled upon him. They were stunned at the sight of Milarepa practicing the "river-flowing" meditation, his eyes fixed, and they ran off in fright. But by and by, cautiously, they returned. Aiming their arrows at the Jetsun, they shouted, "Are you a human or a demon? You look really strange."

Milarepa didn't answer. He continued to sit with a fixed stare. The hunters shot their poisoned arrows at him, but though they aimed carefully, none of them hit. Milarepa didn't move an inch. They tried to burn him with flaming tips but he wouldn't catch fire. So they came closer and threw him bodily over the cliff down the raging river. He went down, stopped just above the water, hovered in full lotus posture, levitated upwards, and returned to his original sitting place. He had still not said a word.

This was too much for the hunters: they took off in a hurry, talking about it all the way back. As they passed a mountain cave, the yogi Chira heard them and exclaimed, "That man was my Lama. He's the greatest yogi in all of Tibet! What you saw is a sign of his accomplishments. He's even taught animals how to meditate!" And

Chira told the hunters a story about a dog and a deer who were spared much suffering thanks to Milarepa. Awed by the story, the hunters spread Milarepa's fame throughout Nepal.

Now the Yerang and Kokom areas were under the control of a king whose ears were pricked by tales of Milarepa. He felt very devoted and even had a vision of Tara[35] telling him, "You have a fine piece of muslin in your treasury. You also have the medicinal myrobalan plant. You should offer these two things to a great tenth-level Bodhisattva, a Tibetan who is now meditating at Katya Cave in southern Nepal. This will augur well."

The king sent an envoy who was fluent in Tibetan. When he found the yogi living like an ascetic, the king's envoy was overwhelmed. *This has got to be Milarepa,* he thought, but just to make sure, he asked, "Lama! What is your name? How do you cope without clothes or food? There's nothing here, don't you need anything?" And the Jetsun said, "I'm Milarepa the Tibetan yogi. No things, no pain. That's how I see it!" And he sang this Song of Happiness Without:

> To all holy Lamas, I bow down!
> I am Milarepa.
>
> These days, I don't care for riches.
> I'm not into acquisitions,
> So I'm not miserable trying to get things at first,
> And I'm not stressed out trying to protect things in the
>   middle,
> And I'm not wretched trying to hold on to things in the end.
> Ownership is no fun: I'm happy without!
>
> These days, I don't care for relations.
> I'm not into emotional games,
> So I'm not miserable with possession at first,
> And I'm not stressed out with arguments in the middle,
> And I'm not wretched from separation in the end.
> Emotional games are no fun: I'm happy without!

These days, I don't care for pride.
I'm not into celebrity,
So I'm not miserable trying to get famous at first,
And I'm not stressed out trying to keep the spotlight in the
    middle,
And I'm not wretched from fear of losing the attention in
    the end.
Celebrity is no fun: I'm happy without!

These days I don't care for countries.
I'm not attached to one place over another,
So I'm not miserable with narrow chauvinism at first,
And I'm not stressed out with patriotic fever in the middle,
And I'm not wretched from defending the homeland in the
    end.
Attachment is no fun: I'm happy without!

THE ENVOY, FILLED with faith, returned to the king and gave him a detailed report. The king was newly inspired and commanded the envoy, "Go back to Milarepa and invite him here. If he won't come, at least give him this muslin and this myrobalan plant."

So the envoy returned to see Milarepa and declared, "The king of Yerang and Kokom is inviting the yogi Milarepa."

"I don't really stay in cities," replied Milarepa, "and I'm not really a sycophant. I'm especially not a yes-man for kings. I don't want fancy meals or fancy goods. It's not a joke that dharma practitioners should endure hunger and cold. It's for real. You go serve your king, I answer only to my Lama Marpa, and that means, I practice. Now you can go back!"

"So a great king sends an envoy for the special purpose of inviting just one yogi, and the yogi won't come?"

"I am the great king!" replied Milarepa. "I am the emperor of the world! There is no king who's happier, richer, or more powerful than I!"

"Oh no?" the envoy retorted. "You know that emperors of the world are supposed to have seven imperial possessions. Show me yours!"

"If you kings and courtiers of the world would follow my way, you'd soon be supreme emperors too, and you'd all be rich and powerful!" And he sang this Song about Being a King:

> To the kings and their courtiers, seekers of pleasure—
> Here's Milarepa's kingdom!
> Follow my lead and you'll be happy,
> For this is Milarepa's kingdom!
>
> Faith is my precious wheel
> Day and night spinning virtue.
>
> Primordial awareness is my jewel
> Fulfilling the wishes of self and others.
>
> Ethics is my queen
> The most beautiful of adornments.
>
> Meditative stability is my minister
> Gathering stores of merit and wisdom.
>
> A sense of decency is my royal elephant
> Bearing the load of the Buddha's teachings.
>
> Diligence is my royal horse
> Leading deluded emotions into selflessness.
>
> Study and contemplation are my generals
> Battling the enemy of erroneous views.
>
> If you have these too,
> You deserve the fame and glory of a king,
> You deserve victory over negative deeds,

You deserve to be served by the ten virtues,
And you deserve to be respected by all mother-beings.

"OH, THAT IS so true to the dharma!" said the envoy. "Look, yogi, if
you don't want to come, then please accept these two gifts from the
king." And he placed the muslin and the myrobalan in Milarepa's
hands. The Jetsun made a wishful prayer of dedication.

AT THIS SAME TIME, Rechungpa and Shengom Repa were on their way
with an invitation of their own for their Lama, Milarepa. On the way
they crossed paths with a band of thieves from Nyishang. The thieves
were about to do them in, but Rechungpa and Shengom Repa shouted,
"Please don't kill us, we're yogis!"

"You, yogis?" laughed the bandits. "Only Milarepa is a true yogi.
Arrows can't hit him. Fire won't burn him. Water won't drown him.
We heard that he was thrown off a cliff, and he just levitated back up.
He even refused an invitation from the king of Kokom." It took an
explanation and a bribe, but finally the thieves directed the yogis to
Milarepa.

When they arrived, Rechungpa and Shengom Repa found Milarepa
dressed in the muslin. The myrobalan was on a slab. "How are you,
Jetsun?" asked the disciples.

"I'm well, I'm extremely well," replied Milarepa, and he sang this
song:

> In this land, flowers bloom,
> Trees stir and sway,
> Birds burst in a thousand songs
> And monkeys fool around.
> I'm happy I found this solitary place,
> Happy that the Lama sits on my head.
> Happy too from the blaze of inner heat,
> The practice of illusory body,
> The self-liberation of the eight worldly concerns.
> Happy I am, when dreamland confusion dissolves naturally,

When clear light dispels the darkness of ignorance.
Happy in enlightenment itself without the need for trans-
ference meditation,
Happy to cut through the bardo,
And abide in the sphere of pure bliss.
That's how happy your old Lama is!
I enjoy the sweet fruits of the wild,
And the cool mountain stream.
Think of what I just said, you will understand.

But tell me, did bandits try to rob you?
If they did, reflect on your karma.

Have no money, you'll make no enemies.
My children, don't ever long for possessions.

Tame your mind, you'll have no enemies.
My children, don't ever start hating.

Know your mind, you'll find no enemies.
My children, see the face of the deity.

Spark compassion, you'll create no enemies.
My children, always care for others.

SHENGOM REPA SAID, "Yogi Jetsun, it's because you have no enemies
that we've come to invite you. You don't need to stay here all alone.
Please come to Tibet for the benefit of beings."

"When I stay here all alone, I bring tremendous benefit to beings,"
replied Milarepa. "Even if I came to Tibet I'd continue to stay in natural retreats. It's not a bad thing, you know. My Lama told me to do
this, and solitude is best for progressing in the different stages of
yoga. Solitude is excellent for developing inner heat. That's how a
yogi sees it. You should do solitary retreat yourself!" And Milarepa
sang this Song of True Style:

I haven't yet repaid my Lama's kindness,
I haven't yet freed all sentient beings.
I practice with a grateful heart,
And it's not that I lack for anything:
It's my oath as an adept.

The wild burro in the north has a white jaw
And never bends his head, not even when he's dying.
It's not that he's looking for a way out—
He is wild—it's just his style.

The tigress in the south is a carnivore
But she never eats her own kind, not even when she's starving.
She doesn't have to be that way—
She's a beast of prey—it's just her style.

The white lioness in the west
Stays in the mountains even when she's freezing.
It's not that she's stuck there—
She's a steadfast animal—it's just her style.

The great vulture in the east
Scythes the air with his wings.
It's not that he's afraid of falling:
Soaring in the sky is just his style.

Milarepa meditates constantly
And gives up the things of this world.
He's not a phony wanting to get famous:
Turning away from attachment is just his style.

Yogis who are fully liberated
Still wander in natural retreats here and there.
It's not that they're afraid to get entangled—
They're accomplished masters—it's just their style.

Monks and students get together
And practice as they've been taught.
It's not that they want to be number one:
Advancing on the path of liberation is just their style.

For you faithful disciples here today,
I've sung a song of oral instructions.
It's not just to pass the time:
It's the style of our lineage.

RECHUNGPA SAID, "JETSUN, you are truly special, there's no other one like you. I'll keep this teaching in my heart. Tell us, who gave you this muslin cloth and this myrobalan plant?" So the Jetsun sang this Song of Gods and Men:

The kingdom of Kokom
Is ruled by a noble man,
A Bodhisattva.
Tara gave him a prophecy:
He should invite Milarepa
Who's meditating in the Katya Cave of Nepal.
But I'm mindful of death, I chose not to go.
So the Nepalese king
Gave me this muslin of soft cotton,
It's a good friend to my inner heat.
I also received this medicinal plant, the myrobalan,
Which cures imbalances of the elements.
So for the next seven years,
There'll be no illness in the kingdom.

RECHUNGPA AND SHENGOM REPA started speaking both at once. "We're going to steer clear of the eight worldly concerns and we're going to practice. Please hold us in your heart!" said the one as the other pleaded, "Please come to Tibet for the sake of sentient beings."

Milarepa agreed and settled at Nyenön Cave in Chudo (Lashi region). The goddess Tseringma wandered through as the Jetsun was enjoying himself with wild women in a grove of teak, but he caught sight of her in a silver mirror and saw her vanish into thin air.

A year later, he was staying at Chölung when Tseringma wandered through again. The Jetsun was riding a lion, his body smeared with saffron, holding a garland of flowers. He was wearing robes of sun and moon and in his hands he held a canopy and a victory banner. She saw she had no chance to play mischief. And this is where we end the story of a gift from the king of Kokom followed by a brief intrusion by Tseringma.

10

YOU WANT TO ARGUE?

Namo guru!

SINCE HE'D GAINED CONTROL over his own perceptions, the Jetsun Milarepa also overpowered external phenomena. The great Indian Darma Bodhi even came to pay him homage. Milarepa was famous.

At Belly Cave in Nyanang, the locals brought him offerings on behalf of both the living and the dead. With increasing good fortune, Milarepa practiced for the sake of beings.

But his success was deeply resented by teachers of the local philosophy school. They spread vicious rumors that he was a false teacher. They slandered him. It was a smear campaign.

When a famine broke out in Nyanang, the locals went to the school looking for loans to make ends meet. But they were told loans were out of the question; the school used gifts only for dharma practice; the school couldn't help; the school had no false teachers; the school never took offerings on behalf of the dead or the living; and why didn't they try their heretic teacher who'd received so much from them.

A couple of the villagers admitted that in a sense the school was right. Taking refuge in the Jetsun for future lives was one thing, but needs in this life were another. It was agreed: they would make offerings to the school as well.

MEANWHILE, THE SCHOOL ELDERS, Lotön Gendun Bum (called Lotön), and Ratön Darma Lodrö (nicknamed Darlo), called a council. The issue was put on the table. "If we don't expel Milarepa, what will happen to our study programs? How we will bring in new students? His propaganda is not the dharma, expelling him is the right thing to do."

"No, no! If we drive him out, there'll be too much talk in town. Here's a better idea: let's take three of our best minds—scholars who know the scriptures and discourses front to back—to challenge him. Milarepa has a tongue but not much else, he won't know how to answer. We throw him a hundred questions, he might have a few comebacks at best. We'll pulverize him with ridicule. He'll be so devastated, he'll run out of town!"

THIS, THEN, WAS the plan. Three scholars were picked and sent off to find Milarepa. When Rechungpa saw them coming, he thought, *They want to meet the Jetsun, I don't like it.* He ran to Milarepa and advised him of the situation, "Should I let them in? Maybe I should tell them not to come?"

Milarepa replied, "My Lama Marpa told me to do good for beings by using my body, my speech and my mind. He said I should even benefit them through ordinary conversation. Bring in the scholars!"

The scholars were brought in. After they'd been given refreshments, Milarepa opened the discussion by saying, "The power of faith can cut open the earth. It can split rocks. It can part the waters. So. In honor of the sutras, please give me a teaching."

The scholar closest to Milarepa stood up. He snapped his fingers to indicate he would argue. "You have here three great scholars," he began. "We philosophize, we meditate, we're knowledgeable. We wear the full monastic robes, as you can see. As for the sutras, maybe I'll give you a teaching, maybe not. But really I'd rather talk about you: you receive lots of gifts and food from the locals. You even look proud of it. How do you justify that?"

In answer, the Jetsun sang the Song of Realizations from Practice:

The ultimate essence of the dharma quest
Is the ambrosia of the oral instruction
As well as the pith of the logic
Which you scholars venerate like a crown jewel.
May this ever adorn my head!

I can explain my practice under three topics,
One dealing with yidam generation,
The next relating to the channels, energy flow and seed es-
    sence in the body,
And the third on Mahamudra meditation.

At the four times of day and night, I arouse bodhichitta.
To expand ultimate faith, I contemplate emptiness
For more exoteric faith, I dedicate tormas
To enhance my own faith, I offer to the deities
The leftovers I give to the elemental spirits.
I'm a yogi, I spin the wheel of offerings.
I know offerings have no true nature,
So I have no problems receiving them.

THE SCHOLAR HAD SAT down again. Now he said, "Imagine a cripple trying to do rock-climbing. That's what it's like if you haven't completed your studies—you won't reach liberation. Now imagine a blind man trying to see things in a temple. That's what it's like if you haven't practiced meditation—you won't get the picture." The second scholar added, "Everyone needs a technique to generate visualizations in their practice. You mentioned yidam generation before. What can you tell us about that?"

In response, Milarepa sang this Song on Generating the Yidam:

When I meditate on visualizing a yidam deity,
My body is like a rainbow in the sky of appearance-emptiness
But without fixation, so there's no clinging.
My speech is like an echo in the valley of sound-emptiness

But without right or wrong, so there's nothing accepted,
   nothing denied.
My mind is like sun and moon beams in the space of light-
   emptiness
But without reference points, so there's no self-centeredness.

Body, speech and mind in the ordinary sense
Arise naturally as vajra body, vajra speech and vajra mind.

In their ordinary form, they're gone—I feel good!
My actions agree with the dharma—I feel happy!
My path is the dharma—I like it!

"WELL, MAYBE," SAID one of the scholars. "What about your explanation on the channels, energy flow and seed essence in the body? I'd
like to hear that."

So Milarepa sang this Song about Meditation on the Channels, Energy Flow and Seed Essence:

There are three main channels and four chakras.
I let go of all clinging to the body—it seems to dematerialize,
The physical elements dissolve into letters that blaze nonstop.

I see the face of reality, no mistake there.
The vital energy is drawn into the central channel and hits
   the spot.
White and red come together,
And here is sudden experience: blissful, luminous, non-con-
   ceptual.

The knots of doubt are undone for good.
That's real dharma, not token dharma.
That's like a mother and her child united again—it's luminous.
The complex defiled by craving is past.

Appearance and emptiness merge into one—I feel good!
Emptiness is no longer an object of thought—I feel happy!
Confusion has been spent in space—I like it!

BUT ONE OF THE SCHOLARS was already talking back, "I want to point out that marmots hibernate four months a year, using a single cycle of their energy flow. They're asleep, they don't stir one bit. I'll also draw your attention to the energy in fish: they can stay underwater and don't need to come up for air. In both these cases, you could say these creatures have a certain skill with their energy flow, yet you can't say that they have any mental skill. I wonder if you're not in the same category! Mental skill is essential, and I'm curious to hear you talk about Mahamudra meditation."

Milarepa responded with a Song on Mahamudra:

When I meditate on Mahamudra,
I rest without effort in the natural state
I rest undistracted in a relaxed state
I rest lucid in emptiness
I rest aware in bliss
I rest easy in non-thought
I rest unperturbed in diversity.

This very mind which rests as I just said
Is a mosaic of knowledge in an endless display
Brought to light just like that, the easy way.
No more hunger for results—I feel good!
No hopes and fears, no duality—I feel happy!
Confusion flashing as wisdom—I like it!

BUT AGAIN THE SAME scholar spoke, "The only worthwhile thing that's come out of your mouth is your tongue! You're not that bad, it's just that you're a mimic, not the real thing. Who's your Lama, by the way?"

Milarepa said, "I study my own mind. I take all appearances as a book. I don't divorce myself from appearances, so I'm never without a book. Appearances are mind and mind is luminous. That's the point, that's my Lama, that's all my Lamas." And he sang, Who is My Lama:

Who is my Lama? He's noble,
His body is the pure land.
For a lion's throne he has five currents,
For a lotus cushion he has five channels,
For a sun-moon seat he has the five elements.
My Lama's body is mind-emptiness.
He is Vajradhara,[36] the embodiment of wisdom,
He is Tilopa,[37] gifted with six supernormal powers,[38]
He is Naropa with the net of magical illusion,
He is Marpa of unequalled kindness.
That's my guru, sitting always on top of my head.
If you're sincere, if you have eyes to see,
You'll recognize that my Lama is none other than Vajradhara.
If you're respectful, if you can pray,
You'll feel the steady rain of his blessings.
If you're generous, if you practice,
The treasury of attainments will open for you.

THE THREE SCHOLARS couldn't help themselves: with this song, they fell in awe of Milarepa. All three rose and prostrated themselves at his feet. One said, "I think of the line, 'Misunderstanding, ignorance and confusion: how these three have harmed the world!' What a true saying. In our ignorance, we mistook you for a rogue profiting from gifts by the locals. But you had persuasive answers to all our questions."

"Yes," continued the second scholar, "we want to apologize for trying to get you into an argument. We haven't had a chance to meet your Lamas, but we've met you, and you're even greater than the *Treasury of Siddhis*, so our sincere prayers will go to you. Would you be so kind as to give us an oral instruction, please?" And his two companions joined in earnest in the request. Milarepa welcomed their respect and set them to meditate with empowerments and oral instructions. The three of them developed excellent realizations and became known as the Three Realized Snow Lions, a.k.a. the Meditating Scholars.

Meanwhile, the locals of Nyanang were preparing for a big feast. They wanted Milarepa to come along with his disciples and the three meditating scholars. They erected a throne for Milarepa and prepared seats for his students. They also built thrones for the two elders of the school, Lotön and Darlo; and finally they arranged rows of seats up front for the school monks.

The meditating scholars showed up wearing the plain cotton loincloth that Milarepa's students wore. They drank liquor from the skullcups as fast as it was served. This sight did not agree with Lotön and Darlo. His face distorted with anger, Lotön seared to Darlo, "That man is a degenerate. A traitor. If that man stays here, our school suffers. Look at what he's done! He's an absolute disgrace. He's got to go. No other way." He turned his wrath on the Jetsun and mocked, "You, yogi! You're really unique. You must have an amazing grasp of logic. I mean, if you didn't, you wouldn't dare have your students drink so freely. Because, you know, it sure looks like you're destroying the Buddhist teachings with that kind of behavior. It sure looks like you're doing no one a favor. It sure looks like you've broken your vows. So please, give me a logical explanation, I'd like to understand."

The Jetsun replied, "Hey scholar, why don't you relax? Release your clutch on the conventional. Rest in naked reality. If you're not meditating, you ought to keep your emotions in check. You must cultivate the natural state from within. Otherwise, you'll fall prey to jealousy and other such poisons, which will send you straight to the lower realms. You'll kill yourself if you go on like this. I don't get your system of logic. My logic is the Lama and the oral instruction. My logic is born of meditative experience and refined through perseverance in solitude. It's the logic of faithful patrons and genuine offerings. Of course, there's also the logic of greed and jealousy: they lead to hell and suffering. I know of no other logic. If you need a

more complete explanation, listen to my song." And he sang the Song
of If Not, Then How:

> At the feet of my untroubled Lama, I bow down!
> How jealousy rears its ugly head these days.
> Lotön, Darlo, listen here!
>
> If I didn't come from my mother's womb,
> How could I have fed from her?
> If I hadn't fed from her,
> How could I have eaten solids?
> If I hadn't eaten solids,
> How could I have grown?
> If I hadn't grown,
> How could I have left home?
> If I hadn't left home,
> How could I have wandered through the land?
> If I hadn't wandered through the land,
> How could I have met my Lama?
> If I hadn't met my Lama,
> How could I have received the ear-whispered instructions?
> If I hadn't received the ear-whispered instructions,
> How could I have endured solitary meditation?
> If I hadn't endured solitary meditation,
> How could I have seen signs of meditative realization?
> If I hadn't seen signs of meditative realization,
> How could I have survived in the cold?
> If I hadn't survived in the cold,
> How could patrons feel inspired by me?
> If patrons didn't feel inspired by me,
> Why should you be jealous, Lotön?
> If you aren't jealous,
> Why should you go to hell?
>
> In this mountain meadow,
> Antelopes run and lark.

But have you seen the wolves?
They're greedy and cunning,
It makes them rabid.

In the Belly Cave of Nyanang,
I, worthy Milarepa, stay.
Have you looked at yourself, teacher of words?
You're green with envy,
Isn't that why you're raging?

I have devoted patrons
And you have a jealous mind.
Have you looked at yourself, learned scholar?
You're full of spleen.
Have you looked at yourselves, teachers?
You're mistaking empty words for the truth.
It's piffle, it's bilge, it's drivel, it's jargon,
Anyone can do it.
Chasing words and labels,
What a waste of a life!

I fight the monster of selfishness—
I don't tinker with words, words, words.
I don't develop complex arguments.
You know better logic?
Fine, you're the winner today.

"NOW, NOW," SAID DARLO. "My colleague asked you for a technical answer and it seems you've not given us one. Your song is very good for brainwashing ignorant folks who can't tell the difference, but I'm not buying it. I'm still waiting for a proper answer. If you're unable to respond with technical terms but insist on receiving alms from the poor people—whom you deceive with your songs—I'm afraid we'll have no choice but to clamp down on you. A kind of temporary suspension." On these words, Darlo bent to the ground. He picked up a handful of dirt and threw it straight at Milarepa's eyes.

The Jetsun wiped his face and smiled. "So that's your dharma, great teacher. You really have a vested interest in your books and your privileged life. You blow an evil wind, and your higher learning will only increase your burden of misery. I see the dharma as a teaching to overcome afflictive emotions. You see the dharma as a tool to foster afflictive emotions. There's no common ground between our words or our techniques."

Rechungpa had grown increasingly incensed. Finally he could contain himself no more. *I'm not worth a hair on Milarepa's head,* he thought, *but if I don't put down this evil slanderer, I'll be breaking my tantric vows. I've got to shut him up.* Convinced he was doing the right thing, Rechungpa brandished a large stick and threw himself on Darlo. But Milarepa's arm stopped him.

"Rechungpa, my son! Sometimes you're down and out but no money is available. Sometimes you're in pain but none of your friends will take care of you. Sometimes you're in a difficult situation but nothing can help. Be careful not to turn things against yourself. Think, Rechungpa, listen to my song." And Milarepa sang the Song of a Lama's Warning:

> You're my crown, kind Marpa,
> At your feet, protector of beings, I bow down!
> Grant your blessings that I may see adverse conditions as
>   the path.
>
> Calm down Rechungpa, listen to me.
> Some practitioners are bloated in every way,
> But when times are tough, there's nothing impressive about
>   them:
> They lose their temper, they're mean and obnoxious.
> Don't pick fights! It's bad news.
>
> Relax Rechungpa, listen to me.
> Think of the dharma view as the sky.

Raise your wings, my little eagle of awareness,
Don't lose your skill,
Or you'll fall in the abyss of prejudice.

Rechungpa, listen to your Lama's warning.
Think of dharma meditation as an ocean.
Swim, my little fish of awareness,
Don't lose your skill,
Or you'll get caught in the net of delusion.

Rechungpa, listen to your Lama's warning.
Think of dharma conduct as a glacial peak.
Limber up, my little cougar of awareness,
Don't lose your skill,
Or you'll go blind in the blizzard of the mundane.

Rechungpa, listen to your Lama's warning.
Think of dharma fruition as a treasure island.
Venture on, my little merchant of awareness,
Don't lose your skill,
Or you'll let slip the gem of reality.

Rechungpa, listen to your Lama.
Don't get so worked up, it's your mind that gets burned.
Don't be so on edge, moderate yourself.

THIS SONG TOOK the sting out of Rechungpa's anger. The consensus among the patrons was that the scholars had been wrong, that Rechungpa had also been somewhat wrong, and that the Jetsun was more than ever worthy of respect. The feast came to an end and they all returned home.

Lotön and Darlo were not pleased. In trying to ridicule Milarepa, they had only ridiculed themselves. By the next morning, they'd planned their revenge. With the help of a few monks from their school, they packed books and dried meat and went to see Milarepa "to offer our apologies," as they said. Rechungpa heard them out and said, "No need to apologize, no reason for further debate, no need to meet the Jetsun." But as he was trying to push them out, a couple of monks slipped in behind his back and asked Milarepa directly if he would see the elders. Milarepa was gentle, he replied, "If you've done wrong you should come clean. But really, the best is if you do no wrong in the first place. The elders? Sure, bring them in."

Darlo and Lotön came in and placed their offerings in front of Milarepa. "This is for you," one of them said. "Yesterday you were right and we were wrong, we're sorry. Let's discuss the dharma again; in fact, we've brought some books for reference. And this time, let's not fight."

The Jetsun replied, "There's an old saying, 'You can tell if a man has eaten or not by the flush on his cheeks.' It's the same here, you can tell if a man knows the dharma or not by the extent of his self-centeredness. Can he master his neurotic emotions? If he can, it's a sign that he's practiced and knows the dharma.

"You may be the best polemicist, the best arguer, but still you rise to the bait," continued Milarepa. "If you're subject to ego-clinging and neurotic emotions, your magniloquence and rhetoric only make you more selfish, more puffed-up. That's what makes samsara go round and round, that's what makes for a hellish life. That's why these debates-for-show are futile. I thank you for your apology. Now the discussion is over. Please go home."

But Darlo would not leave so easily. "Excuse me," he said, "but who are you? Only the Buddha can tell if ego-clinging and neurotic emotions have been overcome. Maybe I am still subject to them, but that doesn't mean that my magniloquence and rhetoric, as you call them, keep me spinning round and round in samsara. You might as well say that knowledge is evil. But for the sake of argument, let's even accept that knowledge is evil: the fact that you say so doesn't mean you're all pure—maybe your naïvete is causing a lot of harm? Maybe your attitude is a bit holier-than-thou? Who knows if that's not an even straighter road to hell! You see, it's necessary to distinguish and discriminate. It's necessary to argue. And I know the rules for an argument." Darlo was on a roll. "Ask any dharma question you want, yogi, and I'll judge whether it's a good one or a bad one. Or I'll even offer you an alternative: if you don't believe that we're learned, then test us with a question, we'll answer. Deal?"

The Jetsun said, "You're not giving me much of a choice. But all right." He looked at the assembled students and monks, and said, "Everyone here knows you, Darlo, and myself, Milarepa. They've seen us both, they've heard us both. I won't ask a big question, I won't ask a small one either. I'll make my case and let you respond. Now answer me, does space obstruct?"

"What kind of a question is that? Anyway, I told you I'd answer, so here's my answer: no, space does not obstruct, it's non-obstructing, what else?"

"Well I say that space does obstruct," Milarepa said.

"What's your basis for saying so?"

Milarepa entered into the samadhi of "Solidified Vajra Space."

"Now," he said, "let's see if space obstructs or not. Please stand up and move around."

But Darlo was as if paralyzed. He couldn't move a limb if his life depended on it. He was fixed in his sitting position and couldn't even open his mouth. Meanwhile, the Jetsun stirred in space, walked, laid down, sat in the vajra posture and did all sorts of tricks. When he emerged from his samadhi, he declared, "You said space does not obstruct. What was it that obstructed your movements, then?"

"It's your voodoo!" accused Darlo. "Evil spells and black magic! If it weren't for your witchcraft, space would not obstruct. The first person off the street will tell you that."

"Is that right? So the first person off the street, without giving it a second thought, will tell me that space does not obstruct? And animals? Do they see it that way as well? Let's face it, I've just discredited you. Who cares if black magic was used? It doesn't change the fact that space can obstruct. But here's my new question." He pointed to large rock in the cave. "You see this rock here? Tell me, is it non-obstructing?"

"So long as you don't start on your magic spells, then a rock is an obstructing thing."

"You said earlier that I could test you. Well, I'm testing you now. I think you're incapable of magic. I challenge you to show me that this rock can become non-obstructing."

"Knowing magic and doing magic are two separate things. You just like to play the witch-doctor to turn people's heads."

"And I thought there was nothing you didn't know!" said Milarepa with irony. "Right now there are countless enlightened beings doing exactly the kind of 'magic' I'm asking you to do—they perform it like rainfall."

The second elder, Lotön, had been silent, but suddenly he spoke up. "All right, you showed us that space can obstruct. Show us now that this rock does not obstruct, yogi."

The Jetsun entered into the samadhi of "Decomposed Space." He passed through the rock and came out the other side, then did it again. He passed through it from top to bottom. He put half his body in it. He went on like this for a while, and finished by throwing the rock up in the air, allowing it to fall on him, picked it up with his hand, said to Rechungpa, "Bring me a large pole!" and placed the rock on top of it. He even left his handprints on the rock. You can still see them today.

Lotön was very intrigued. "It's pretty clear you made this rock non-obstructing. What I don't understand is, if it's not magic, then I should be able to do it too, right?"

"Oh yes, you could do it too," said Milarepa. "If it was obstructing, I don't think I'd be alive now, not after it fell on me!"

But Darlo returned to the discussion, insisting, "I didn't feel any rock. Of course, [ultimately] a rock does not exist, so [ultimately] it does not obstruct. What else is new?"

"That just proves my point," said Milarepa. "It didn't touch you because it did not obstruct. Just because you don't feel something doesn't mean it doesn't exist."

By this time, Darlo was apoplectic, but Lotön was beginning to have doubts. *It seems real enough*, he thought. *I'm a skeptic, but what if this was more than magic? He just may be a realized yogi. I should ask him to teach on the six perfections.* Which he did. Milarepa replied with a song:

> Buddha, dharma, sangha, you're my royal refuge,
> I make a heartfelt prayer
> That you may always crown my head
> Like a radiant ornament.
> Embrace me with your compassion!
> Love all beings on the way to ultimate truth.
>
> In Mahayana yoga, there's no claptrap dharma to be heard,
> In genuine emptiness, there's no thought to be had,
> In the truth of no arising, there's no meditation to practice.
> That's how I give up evil.
>
> If you can't loosen the knot of greed,
> Why talk about generosity?
>
> If you can't reject sham and lies,
> Why pretend morality?
>
> If you can't control your virulence,
> Why harass us with your patience?
>
> If you can't reject laziness and apathy,
> Why insist on perseverance?
>
> If you can't quell your busy mind,
> Why strain yourself in meditation?
>
> If you can't see that appearances are your friends,
> Why practice wisdom?
>
> If you can't fathom assent and denial,
> Why bother with studies?

If you can't qualify to do and not to do,
Why explain cause and effect?

If you can't fit your mind to the dharma,
Why put on your monk's robes?

You can't slash the snake of neurotic emotions?
Then your ideal of wisdom is delusion.

You can't ease your spasms of jealousy?
Then your ideal of bodhichitta is delusion.

You can't stop hurting others?
Then your ideal of respect is delusion.

You can't help bringing everything back to yourself?
Then your ideal of impartiality is delusion.

Unless you subdue the demon of ego-clinging,
Your neurosis will destroy your yoga.

Unless your actions are consistent,
You'll sabotage the attempts of others.

Unless your mind embraces the dharma,
You'll confuse others with your hype.

So focus on meditation—
You may die tomorrow.

"OK, SO YOU'VE HEARD of the six perfections," conceded Darlo. "What about the ten perfections?"[39]
    So Milarepa sang this song:

Kind translator Marpa,
Protect beings in these degenerate times,
Grant your blessings that jealousy may be pacified.

Listen Darlo, Mr. Pretension.
For the last thirty-two years,
You've done nothing but argue;
You haven't thought about death once.
But there's still hope for you if you start to practice!
These are dark days, beings are terribly afflicted,
It's so easy for a few snakes to deceive them.

I've crossed to the shore of no ego:
There's no distinct generosity!

I've crossed to the shore of no deceit:
There's no distinct morality!

I've crossed to the shore of fearless truth:
There's no distinct patience!

I've crossed to the shore of radical practice:
There's no distinct perseverance!

I've crossed to the shore of intimate stillness:
There's no distinct meditation!

I've crossed to the shore of the natural state:
There's no distinct awareness!

I've crossed to the shore of perfection:
There's no distinct skillful means!

I've crossed to the shore of victory over evil:[40]
There's no distinct power!

I've crossed to the shore good for self and others:
There's no distinct prayer!

Deluded emotions are great awareness:
There is no distinct wisdom!

That's the genuine way to practice,
Let's not waste words.

THE SECOND ELDER, Lotön, had been in doubt for a while, but this song sealed his conviction in Milarepa. "Yes!" he exclaimed, "that's the way! Your meditation and your experience are truly great, yogi!"

But Darlo was indignant, "Your talk is parrot-talk, Milarepa! It can't withstand analysis. And your voodoo magic? Standard witch-doctor tricks. As far as your little song on the ten perfections, that's all superficial—it's completely inconsistent with these books right here. Why don't we talk about what the books say?" Darlo pointed to the pile by his side, "One must come to a rigorous understanding of logic. Logic is fundamental. If you have a good grasp of logic, all the other stuff comes second. So let's begin: I'm going to ask you a question, and I'll have no problems giving you credit if you can answer it. Now. Let's look at generally characterized phenomena. More specifically, in terms of cognition we speak of both direct perception and inference. There are false reasonings, logical reasonings and undetermined reasonings. That's the basic philosophical tenets. What do you say to that?"

"Teacher, teacher," said the Jetsun, "what kind of demons have gotten into you? You don't trust your own mind, you don't trust your yidam deity, you don't even seem to trust the Buddha, so I'm not surprised you don't trust me. There's one kind of dharma that you really like, it's the foul dharma-soup of withered compassion and dried renunciation. One sip of it and my tongue starts to burn, my stomach bloats with pride. The bilge of narcissism rises to my throat and I vomit chunks of jealousy. What's left descends my bowels, I fart the stink of spite and shit big turds of arrogance. Ugh! I've got the virus of malevolence.

"No, I'm not into your nasty dharma. It's perverse. I know for a fact that appearances are no different than mind and that mind is luminous emptiness. So I have no interest in double dealings. And this is my direct experience, not an 'inference.'

"You asked for reasonings? Your perceptions run counter to the dharma—that's a perfect example of 'false reasoning.' And your perceptions feed into your afflictions—there's a fine example of 'logical reasoning.' Last but not least, as a dharma poseur, you present both false and logical characteristics—that's a good example of 'undetermined reasoning.'"

Lotön had to hide in his robes to keep himself from laughing. Darlo's hands were shaking, but suddenly a smile appeared on his lips. "Ha ha ha, I laugh! How thoughtful of you to set me on the right path! You wouldn't know one end of my shit from the other, but who cares, you're the Buddha himself, right? Oh, you're very funny. Let's review your pearls of wisdom: you said demons had gotten into me. Can you confirm this? Then you said I was narcissistic and arrogant, presumably because I'm a scholar. But are you any different? You take yourself for the Buddha, you even humiliate me. And that's the extent of your logic. Well. You're really worthless. You haven't even properly answered my question. Instead, you show off with useless talk as if you're trying to prove that your dick is bigger than a donkey's. Please, control yourself and shut your mouth."

"I was happy sitting with my mouth shut but you had to barge in," said the Jetsun. "I can see that you don't care for my method, but I do: for me it's a source of happiness. I know what I said embarrassed you, and I know it looked like I was boasting. But see, in all sentient beings, mind is luminous emptiness—it's affected neither by samsara's flaws nor by nirvana's grace. This fundamental consciousness is called enlightenment, or Buddha nature. But due to ignorance—which is only an adventitious stain—we fail to recognize it, so we live through the cycles of samsara and we're deluded beings. When we do recognize this fundamental consciousness as primordial awareness, we've reached nirvana and we're fully enlightened Buddhas.[41] Shakyamuni Buddha said, 'Buddha nature is present in all beings. All beings without exception are Buddhas.' He also said, 'All beings are Buddhas. A Buddha is a being without adventitious stains [on his consciousness].' It's also said that when you realize your own mind, you are the very essence of awareness and there's no other Buddha to look for. Meditate on this supreme teaching. If you realize original luminous emptiness, you are enlightened. That's why my method is all about realizing my own mind. You, teacher, don't believe in that obviously.

"And about demons that have gotten into you," Milarepa now said, "I can prove it right in front of everybody here, but it's really too embarrassing, so let's let it be."

"Oh, you're really amazing!" said Darlo. "Well go on, you've got proof? Show us! Demons or not, I'm sure I'm not half as evil as a person I know who brainwashes others with his voodoo magic."

The Jetsun smiled. "If you say so. It's your call. Listen here. There's something that you're really attached to, and yet you passed it to someone else. Is that a sign of demons or what?"

Darlo's face turned pale. But Rechungpa was already up and, ignoring Milarepa's attempts to stop him, went straight to a beautiful girl (she didn't believe in Milarepa much but she was devoted to Rechungpa) and unhooked a bracelet off her wrist, which Darlo had given to her. He showed it for all to see. Darlo now turned crimson with shame and could find nothing to say. When his tongue returned, he heaped abuse on Milarepa and Rechungpa and walked out. Rechungpa was having a grand time of it all, passing the bracelet around. Next he went to the girl's place and retrieved a rosary that Darlo had also given her. Witnesses were completely convinced of Darlo's corruption.

The second elder, Lotön, thought to himself, *Now hold on! If no one told Milarepa about this, he must be the real thing. Still, I'd like definitive proof.* He gathered up the books that Darlo, in his anger, had left behind, and said his goodbyes with the words, "Enough arguments for one day."

THAT VERY EVENING, Lotön filled up his begging bowl with blood and poured milk into the skullcup used for his rituals. Then he turned upside down his pictures of Buddhas and Bodhisattvas. *If Milarepa knows I've done that,* he thought, *then he's got supernatural powers and he's really enlightened.* The next day, Lotön returned to see Milarepa but on the way he met Rechungpa who exclaimed, "Well, if that isn't Lotön! You're planning to smear the dharma again—and yourself in the process?"

"No, I've come to pay my respects to the Lama," replied Lotön, who walked right past Rechungpa and went in to see Milarepa. The Jetsun smiled at Lotön and said, "You really don't need to test me like this. I know your secrets, you see. You poured blood—the essence of the five poisons—into your monk's bowl, and you filled your ritual skullcup with the milk normally used for your bowl. You also inverted your pictures. On purpose. Please don't be so irreverent. Go pour the right liquids into the right containers and turn your Buddha images the right way up."

Lotön was so awed he was dumbfounded. He felt immense respect for Milarepa. "I want to learn your dharma!" he said. "I'm a believer now!"

"I'm glad you're inspired," said Milarepa. "But I mustn't waste my teachings on a student who's not really responsive." And he sang this song of Secret Teachings:

> At your feet, translator Marpa, I bow down!
> Grant your blessings that this beggar may keep the secret word.
>
> Tantra is secret and mighty,
> On a pedant like you, it's a waste.
>
> No matter how deep the meditation,
> On a big mouth like you, it's a waste.
>
> Secret tantra must be practiced secretly.
> On a peacock like you, it's a waste.

Bodhichitta is for true yogis.
On bureaucrats, it's a waste.

Oral teachings are passed to worthy students,
On the wrong person, it's a waste.

Sticking to solitude at first
Only to abandon it later, that's a waste.

This yogi's song of experience is deep,
But if shared with every man and his brother, it's a waste.

I could go on,
But this should do as an answer.

LOTÖN SAID, "IF YOU don't want to share your inner experience, maybe
you'll agree to tell me about the wisdom that arises from meditation.
Can you sing about the different stages of the path, and about view,
meditation, conduct and fruition?" Milarepa said, "I don't know your
system, but here's how I do it—" and he sang the Song to Lotön:

At your feet, translator Marpa, I bow down!

Listen to my song, Lotön,
And for once, don't jump to conclusions.

Nothing to see, that's the best view—
Mind itself shines bright.

Nothing there, that's the best find—
Mind itself is the treasure.

Nothing to eat, that's the best feast—
You savor the taste of liberating samadhi.

Nothing to drink, that's the best toast—
You imbibe the nectar of bodhichitta.

This self-aware wisdom is beyond words.
It's not about mere personal liberation,
And it's not about sophistry.

If you realize this truth (which is not something given to
  you),
You've got the best of empowerments.

If you realize this truth (which is neither high nor low),
You're at the topmost level.

If you realize this truth (which is not a journey),
You're on the supreme path.

If you realize this truth (which is beyond birth and death),
You've got the *sine qua non.*

If you realize this truth (which cannot be measured),
You're in the best dimension.

If you realize this truth (which is neither great nor small),
You're on the supreme vehicle.

If you realize this truth (which is beyond good and evil),
You've found the perfect method.

If you realize this truth (which is non-dual),
You've got the premium view.

If you realize this truth (which is beyond reference points),
You have the greatest meditation.

If you realize this truth (which neither accepts nor rejects),
You're engaged in the finest work.

If you realize this truth (which is effortless),
You're tasting the most exquisite fruit.

Pretentious teachers can't get this, of course,
Neither can pedantic academics,
And neither can prejudiced meditators.

Liberation is their ideal but bondage their reality.
They're roped by dualism.

Freedom is their ideal but chains their reality.
They're caught in the split between perceiver and perceived.

Out there is their ideal but down here their reality.
Oh, how they sink in samsara's realms.

MILAREPA'S SONG EFFECTIVELY removed the last of Lotön's pride. Lotön prostrated and begged for teachings but was refused. Undeterred, and with intense faith, he said, "This has been a genuine debate. And you have won."

Back at the school, Lotön commented to Darlo that Milarepa was a genuine teacher; that they, the elders, had shown little faith or renunciation, let alone sacred outlook; that whether their knowledge helped or actually hindered their advance towards liberation was really an open question; and that he felt bad about accusing Milarepa of voodoo magic.

"Lotön, don't you ever grow up?" said Darlo. "So now you're a believer! I'm telling you, the man is evil, he's possessed. His supernatural powers *are* witch-doctor tricks. He doesn't know the first thing about the dharma. As for the girl, I never slept with her."

Darlo stuck to his lies. Soon afterwards, he died. His venom caused him to take rebirth as a frightful demon (it was witnessed by others).

Aware of this development, the Jetsun said, "The bad connection Darlo made with me has sent him off the deep end of samsara."

As for Lotön, he put himself at Milarepa's mercy. He was to become one of five good meditators among Milarepa's close son-disciples, as will be shown in a later story.[42]

11

A TEACHING DEEP AND SIMPLE

Namo guru!

THE JETSUN MILAREPA was at Belly Cave in Nyanang when a merchant of the Me clan came to visit him. This merchant, called Megom, was greatly devoted to the Jetsun and offered all his possessions. Megom received instructions to set him on the path, and went to meditate. Before long, he had experiences and realizations. And no sooner had the Jetsun given him a teaching on the union of view, meditation and conduct than he beheld his own original face. Feeling elated, he received a liberating instruction and was preparing a feast to celebrate when the disciple Drigom Repa asked him, "Megom, I'm curious, have you actually gained certainty in the instructions? I mean, do you have signs like inner heat?"

"Oh yes, most definitely, and it's all thanks to the Lama. Whatever comes up, good or bad, doesn't bother me because I have his instruction. I've even made the decision to stay in solitary retreat for good."

The Jetsun heard this and was pleased, "That's the way, Megom! If you have confidence in the Lama and his instruction, you're sure to develop experiences and realizations. If it doesn't happen right away, you must have the will to persevere." And Milarepa sang this Song of Cutting Confusion:

Translator Marpa, at your feet, I bow down!
Megom and all of you gathered here,
Here's the song of an old man with his share of realiza-
   tions.
Think about its meaning, and practice accordingly.
I have cut confusion at the root.

The Lama blazes in me—
Not in you?
Then don't venture without a realized master.

Appearances shine like a sacred text to me—
Not to you?
Then don't think of doing without a holy teaching.

Attachment has been truly reversed in me—
Not in you?
Then don't let your mind off the hook.

I've realized the meaning of no arising—
Not you?
Then don't ignore cause and effect.

I understand that samsara and nirvana are not two—
Not you?
Then meditate on the union of the two truths.

I've refined self and other until they're inseparable—
Not you?
Then develop bodhichitta.

Realizations dawn naturally in me—
Not in you?
Then don't put down analysis.

For me, there's no split between meditation and post-medi-
    tation—
Not for you?
Then you'd better practice your yogas in solitude.

Experience flows like a river in me—
Not in you?
Then don't ignore the main points of practice.

I've realized all the dimensions of enlightenment—
Not you?
Then focus on the union of the generation and completion
    stages.

My senses and consciousness are relaxed and natural—
Yours not?
Then don't do away with your samaya vow.

"OH, JETSUN," EXCLAIMED Megom Repa happily. "How generous of
you! Can you also summarize the instructions on view, meditation
and conduct!"
    And now, Milarepa sang another song:

Homage to my gracious Lama!
What happiness it is to behold the non-dual view,
What delight it is to experience non-dual meditation,
And what bliss it is to have non-dual conduct.
What wonders, these three kinds of non-duality.

If you don't behold the non-dual view,
How can the real or the merely possible be dharma-body?

If you don't experience non-dual meditation,
How can you turn suffering into an ornament?

If you don't perform non-dual conduct,
How can you be truly free of attachment?

The beings of samsara's six realms
And the wisdom of nirvana
Are inseparable. It's a single state.
Abide in this non-dual view.

The various appearances red and white
And the awareness of reality
Are inseparable. It's a single dimension.
Practice this non-dual meditation.

The moon's reflection gives luster all around
The rainbow shines though it's not tangible
The lamp's brightness illuminates all things.
Practice this non-dual conduct.

It's there in all beings,
This unified reality in three different guises.

At heart, the view is non-duality,
Meditation is non-distraction,
Conduct is union,
And fruition is these three unified.
Practice like that, my children!

EVERY ONE OF THE DISCIPLES was enriched by this song. Now, in preparation for his solitary retreat, Megom asked for a teaching deep and simple. The Jetsun said, "Here's something that I found helpful. Try it as well . . ." And he sang the Song of a Teaching Deep and Simple:

I'm the yogi Milarepa,
I look straight at the essence, and I see!

What I see is like the sky, it's not made up.
I'm easy, I've realized the natural state.
I've realized that all things are empty of true nature.
I'm relaxed, all things dissolve of themselves.
I've distilled the stream of awareness.
I'm really a renunciate, I've cut conceptual thoughts.
I'm out of the abyss of samsara's realms.
I've recognized the Buddha as my own mind,
So I'm done with strategies of want.
Realizations dawn within,
Like the sun, they cast out the shadows.
Afflictive emotions, thoughts, concepts:
I don't feed any of them, so they pass.

THIS SONG DELIGHTED Megom. He went to meditate in solitude and showed extraordinary signs including inner heat. He later became one of the close son-disciples of Milarepa and was of great help to other good practitioners.

12

Happy / miserable

Namo guru!

THE JETSUN MILAREPA and his heart-disciple Rechungpa went to India. On the way back, they went to Red Rock, where Milarepa's patrons and main disciples were holding a feast. There, Milarepa foretold the coming of the great Gampopa.[43] Afterwards, he was invited by his patrons in Chubar, and settled there for a time.

At that point, a great meditator from the Len tribe in Dakpo showed up; he was called Lengom. He'd been greatly inspired by what he'd heard of the Jetsun and was determined to meet him. As soon as Lengom set eyes on Milarepa, an excellent meditative experience of bliss and non-conceptuality arose in him. He was filled with the most perfect faith and exclaimed:

"Lama, I'm known as a good meditator from Dakpo. I've received a fair amount of instructions on Dzogchen and all that. I've done a lot of thinking and I've meditated too. I've even experienced the one-taste of all phenomena. But beyond this, I don't feel I've had any experiences or realizations. I heard a lot about you, so here I am, requesting a teaching. Please teach me the dharma!"

In response, the Jetsun Milarepa asked, "Has your practice so far been a bit like this—" and he sang about Missing the Point:

Hung up on mere words,
Have you perhaps missed the Lama's oral instruction?

Focused on duality,
Have you perhaps missed discriminating awareness?

Stuck on perceiver and perceived,
Have you perhaps missed the view that's fully realized?

Stumbling on the path of names and labels,
Have you perhaps missed the meditative concentration free
    of reference points?

Suspended in doubt,
Have you perhaps missed activity that unfolds as one-taste?

Looking to others for results,
Have you perhaps missed the fruit of nirvana?

Clouded like muddy water,
Have you perhaps missed the genuine transmission?

Corrupted by exaggeration and denigration,
Have you perhaps missed natural mind itself, emptiness?

Meditating in solitude, like a yogi,
Have you perhaps been misled by demons in disguise?

In this samsaric ignorance we churn,
Just like a potter's wheel.

"OH LAMA, THAT'S JUST IT!" said Lengom. "Can you please give me
instructions and empowerments so I can change?" The Jetsun did so
and then sent the yogi off to meditate. But the yogi was still limited

by his habit of reification. He thought of going to town, he thought of many things. Finally he returned to Milarepa (who was fully aware of all this) and related his experiences. Milarepa told him, "Let go of your swarming thoughts—'this is virtuous, that's virtuous, I need to go to town'—let go of them all! Get focused! If you don't, you'll stay miserable in samsara." And he sang this Song of Warning:

> If you hold the noble lineage,
> Confusion will dissolve in its own sphere,
> All things will come at the right time.
> That's how it is for a true yogi.

> In Mahamudra meditation,
> There's no need for the mind to cling to labels.
> As for what arises from the state of non-fabrication,
> Why all the chanting? Why all the analysis?

> Yogis who spend their time in town
> Pander to family and friends.
> They act like hypocrites, speak lies
> And cast shadows on awareness-emptiness inseparable.

> Conceptual mind is exhausting—give it up!
> Must you be on your deathbed to feel regret?
> Remember death and impermanence
> And watch out for the demon of neurotic emotions.

> If you don't meditate always in solitude,
> You risk falling in the abyss of the six kinds of beings.

> If you don't look straight at mind,
> You risk becoming dull and vague.

> If you pray to the Lama without much devotion,
> You risk dimming your experiences.

If you don't exert yourself with real effort on the profound
    path of means,
You risk losing out to the enemy of neurotic emotions.

But if you spend your time in solitary retreat,
You'll develop all qualities.

The Jetsun has seen my deepest flaws, thought Lengom. He returned to his solitary meditation, stayed focused, and gave birth to exceptional realizations.

When he told the Jetsun of his experiences, Milarepa was delighted and said, "Very good! Now you need to continue until you've reached full enlightenment. There's a few things you need to stay away from, and a few others you need to develop." And he sang the Song of Abandoning and Cultivating:

A child, a wife, a reputation—
These three shackle a yogi.
A dharma practitioner should abandon them.

Luxury, pleasure, arrogance—
These three are obstacles to a yogi.
A dharma practitioner should abandon them.

Relatives, patrons, disciples—
These three hinder a yogi.
A dharma practitioner should abandon them.

Alcohol, lethargy, sleep—
These three steal from a yogi.
A dharma practitioner should abandon them.

Gossip, giggles, games—
These three distract a yogi.
A dharma practitioner should abandon them.

Lama, pith instruction, faith—
These three give support to a yogi.
A dharma practitioner should cultivate them.

Solitude, supportive friends, subsistence—
These three keep a yogi balanced.
A dharma practitioner should cultivate them.

Non-distraction, non-conceptuality, bliss—
These three keep a yogi company.
A dharma practitioner should cultivate them.

Alertness, ease, spontaneity—
These three define a yogi's attitude.
A dharma practitioner should cultivate them.

No attachment, no anger, but higher perception—
These three are a yogi's signs on the path.
A dharma practitioner should cultivate them.

LENGOM RESPONDED, "JETSUN! Thanks to your kindness, I'm staying away from the bad stuff and working on the good stuff. I'm very happy these days."

"That's good, my son," replied the Jetsun. "A yogi who practices as I advised will indeed be happy. But someone who goes the opposite way will be miserable always. Now I'll tell you the distinction between being happy and being miserable."

And he sang the Song of Happy/Miserable:

Happy is the yogi
Who recognizes his own face
And is in touch with the natural state.
But one who goes down the road of delusion,
Caught in suffering,
Is forever miserable.

Happy is the yogi
Who rests in the unfabricated nature,
For whom all dissolves in its own unchanging ground.
But one who lusts after sensations,
Uncontrollably filled with anger and desire,
Is forever miserable.

Happy is the yogi
Who knows all appearances as dharma-body
And cuts through doubts, hopes and fears.
But one who babbles on stupidly,
At the mercy of the eight worldly concerns,
Is forever miserable.

Happy is the yogi
Who recognizes all things as his own mind
And befriends whatever comes his way.
But one who wastes his life,
Dying heavy with regret,
Is forever miserable.

Happy is the yogi
For whom realizations dawn
Naturally, in the naked state.
But one who thirsts after desire,
Parading, staggering,
Is forever miserable.

Happy is the yogi
Who continually experiences
The self-liberation of labels.
But one who believes in conventional words
Without coming to terms with mind itself
Is forever miserable.

Happy is the yogi
Who abandons mundane aims, fixed ideas
And petty goals.
But one who feathers his nest
For the narrow sake of family and friends
Is forever miserable.

Happy is the yogi
Who's turned away from attachment deep inside,
And perceives all phenomena as illusion.
But one who goes, distracted,
Enslaved by the physical and the verbal,
Is forever miserable.

Happy is the yogi
Who rides the horse of perseverance
And advances on the path of liberation.
But one who is lazy,
Anchored to samsara's depths,
Is forever miserable.

Happy is the yogi
Who listens, reflects and cuts through mental labels
And watches the theatre of mind.
But one who claims the dharma
While engaging in reprehensible behavior
Is forever miserable.

Happy is the yogi
Dwelling always in the natural state
Beyond doubts, hopes and fears.
But one who depends wholly on others,
Always flattering, never rocking the boat,
Is forever miserable.

Happy is the yogi
Who's left behind the busy world
To practice the holy dharma.

THE YOGI LENGOM and Milarepa's other students were greatly energized and uplifted by this song. They settled in an unwavering state
of Mahamudra meditation, and afterwards exerted themselves in developing what is worthwhile and abandoning what is not. Milarepa
was delighted with Lengom, who later became patron, disciple and
dharma brother to the great Gampopa.

13

TO A SCHOLAR

Namo guru!

LOTÖN GENDUN PROSTRATED before Milarepa. Lotön had once studied with Darlo (a teacher who had debated Milarepa),[44] but he was now a student of Rechungpa and Seben Repa.

"Great Jetsun," Lotön said. "I'm so glad to see you again. I saw my friend [Darlo] die, and I'm just not sure if the dharma I practice is the real thing. So I'm here with my faith. Please, *please* give me an instruction to practice."

The Jetsun replied, "You waste a whole lot of time on a whole lot of nothing and you're not mindful of death. I wouldn't call that the real thing." And he sang the Song of Why the Buddha Taught:

> Why did the mighty Buddha teach?
> So people would see through the eight worldly concerns.
> But scholars so full of themselves these days
> Are slave to the eight worldly concerns.
>
> Why did the Buddha teach monastic discipline?
> So people would give up mundane activities.
> But these days monks
> Are taken with mundane activities.

Why did the Buddha teach the ways of the hermit?
So people would stop sucking dry their family and friends.
But these days those who pass for hermits
Are busy putting on a show.

What I'm saying is, unless you're mindful of death,
Your practice (whatever it is) won't add up to much.

LOTÖN SPOKE NOW. "Yes that's me, I'm afraid. Please, *please* tell me how to be mindful of death."

To test Lotön's resolve to practice, the Jetsun declared, "Well, you can always reach enlightenment through the gradual study of philosophy—that is, if you're not attached to this life." And he sang:

Homage to my father Lama!
Listen, great monk:

The basic vow of personal liberation
Holds the house of teachings.
You want this pillar to be straight.

The sutras and logic that you listen to
Polish the gem of teachings.
You need them to remove impure views.

The commitments of the three higher trainings[45]
Protect the Buddhist teachings.
You want them on your side, not against you.

The Mahayana view destroys the arguments of idiots
With its sutras and logic.
You need it to brighten the dim.

NOW LOTÖN REPLIED with urgency, "My practice has been all words. Please, *please* teach me the essential dharma." The Jetsun knew the time had come to give Lotön the *vinaya* teachings on discipline, but he pretended to be in deep thought and sported a frown. So Lotön went and begged Rechungpa, Seben Repa and others to help. They pleaded for him, which delighted the Jetsun who told Lotön, "Thanks to the efforts of your friends, I will give you the instructions. Perhaps you've got the stuff meditators are made of, but if you receive a teaching and don't practice it, then this is what happens—" And he sang the song Watch Out:

> Homage to all noble Lamas!
> You've come pleading, monks and meditators both.
> Our monk Lotön of the local upper class
> Made his request.
> He asked for instructions to engage in the path.
> Noble enough, as are those who pleaded for him.
>
> I'm the yogi Milarepa,
> Cherished son of the enlightened Marpa.
> I'm not just spinning words
> I'm not just in love with the sound of my own voice.
> What I say is meaningful
> What I say comes from the heart
> What I say stands up to analysis.
> So listen now to this old-timer!
>
> If you receive the dharma but fail to meditate,
> You'll be lucky to get reborn as a hungry ghost wandering
>   in space.
> Wandering hungry ghosts know the different classes of
>   tantra.
> They're familiar with rational contradictions
> And know all about conventional logic
> They're good too with the supernatural, the magical
> And enjoy all kinds of pleasures
> Their minds are very sharp.

But they don't actually practice dharma
They're oblivious to cause and effect
They can't give up their arrogance
Can't stop thinking about themselves
They haven't the slightest inkling of emptiness and com-
    passion
They haven't got the raft needed to cross the river of samsara
For them, dissatisfaction isn't about to disappear.
Sure, they know all there is to know! Sure, they're clairvoyant!
But all their conceptual references
Are fire, wood, burning up their consciousnesses.
In the end, they harm themselves with their evil.
Better you practice the dharma!

There's a pill that will revive the dead,
But if it's not taken,
What good will it do?
Better you eat that pill!

The gods have a potion that protects from death,
But for those who aren't gods
And aren't able to partake,
There'll be death for sure, and untimely too.
So what good does the potion do?
If you want to be free from untimely death,
Better you drink the potion!

The lord of death and his minions have a treasure
Known as the banquet of a hundred flavors.
But those who don't taste of it
Will die of hunger.
What good is the banquet then?
If you don't want to go hungry,
Better you taste that banquet.

LOTÖN FELT AN IMMENSE faith and said, "Jetsun, you convince me more
with every word you say. Please, *please* teach me about the six perfections." So Milarepa sang:

> I'm no scholar speaking in hyperboles,
> No preacher I.
> But you're making a sincere request, so . . .
> The entire dharma is in the six perfections:
>
> Generosity is a noble custom.
> If you give away your possessions
> (Which only distract a practitioner),
> You'll be reborn a comfortable god.
>
> Ethics make a ladder to liberation.
> Whether you're a monk or a layman
> You should follow the Buddhist way
> And stick to it.
>
> Patience is the mark of the wise
> And was pursued by the Buddha.
> It's a garment difficult to wear
> But it does you some good.
>
> Perseverance gets you straight to liberation—
> You can't do without it in your practice.
> If you give up, you've got no hope
> So ride the horse of perseverance.
>
> These four dharmas bring you merit,
> They're indispensable.
> Now I'll turn to wisdom.
>
> Meditative stability connects merit and wisdom
> It is the bridge extending

From the one to the other
And it guards you from distractions.

Wisdom is the definitive meaning,
The one treasure of all the Buddhas.
Enjoy it ceaselessly!
It's like a gem—no more scarcity
For sentient beings, any sentient being.

If you can at last let go of your many things to do,
Wisdom will truly give you rest.
It's the jewel
That leads you step by step to enlightenment.
That is my answer to your request.
Take it to heart, think about it, practice it.

LOTÖN FOUND THIS SONG very helpful. Now Milarepa said to his two disciples Rechungpa and Seben Repa, "Prepare the shrine, I'm going to initiate Lotön." When all was ready, Milarepa transmitted many empowerments and oral instructions to Lotön, who gave birth to all kinds of realizations. But one day, as Milarepa was surrounded by throngs of students, Lotön approached the Jetsun and said, "I can't meditate, I get visions and my mind goes all over the place. If it's not good, how do I clear this up? And if it is good, how do I pursue it further?" *He's really been meditating,* thought Milarepa, who answered, "Lotön, whatever comes up is all right. It's not about being good or not good, it's about practicing the view." And he sang this Song of One to Six:

Homage to all the Lamas!
Lotön, and all of you students sitting here,
Do you know how to view appearances?
In case you don't—
All that manifests is appearances
To those who don't realize it, it's samsara

But to those who realize it, it's dharma-body
When appearances manifest as dharma-body
You need no other view.

Do you know how to meditate with a settled mind?
In case you don't—
Engage the mind itself, don't let it scatter
Don't try to adjust it
Rest in your own nature, like a child
Rest beyond the waves, like the ocean
Rest luminous, like a lamp
Rest without pretension, like a corpse
Rest immobile, like a mountain
The mind just is, nothing more, nothing less.

Do you know how experiences arise?
In case you don't—
They arise and dispel darkness, like a strong sun.
You don't need to give up your thoughts.
Experiences arise as in a dream, without basis
They arise like the reflection of the moon in water, beyond
    grasp
They arise like a rainbow, beyond substance
They arise like space itself, beyond direction.

Do you know how to overcome challenges?
In case you don't—
There are strong winds, but always in the atmosphere
There are huge waves, but always in the ocean
There are thick clouds, but always in the sky
There are wild thoughts, but always in the unborn.
Come into the house of awareness
Practice the instruction on mind and energy
And when the crook of conceptual thought shows up,
Practice the instruction on recognizing your true face.

Also, when your mind wanders,
Practice the instruction on watching the albatross fly back
   to the ship.

Do you know how to conduct yourself?
In case you don't—
Stand awesome like a lion
Rise from the mud like a lotus
Act crazy like an elephant
Be polished like a crystal.

Do you know how results dawn?
In case you don't—
Dharma-body springs from non-conceptuality
Enjoyment body from bliss itself
Emanation body from clarity
And the essential body from naked reality.
I've got these four bodies, these four dimensions,
And I don't waver from the sphere of reality.

One, two, three: view, meditation and experiences;
Four, five, six: challenges, conduct and results.
These six shine in me.
Now it's your turn, practice likewise.

LOTÖN FOLLOWED MILAREPA'S advice and continued to exert himself
in meditation. Soon, special experiences and realizations dawned and
he offered this song to the Jetsun:

To all father Lamas, I pay homage!
This clear-light nature of mind knows no birth and no death.
The practice of mind and energy reveals it to be all-pervasive,
Whole and beyond reference points.
Having neither color nor shape, mind is outside the realm
   of the senses.

Having no words for it, it's outside the realm of labels.
Having no conventional concepts for it, it's outside the realm
    of the intellect.

By practicing this profound instruction
The experience of inner heat pervades the body,
And definitive understanding shines within:
I've cut through the external imputations placed on appear-
    ances.
Failure to develop the path of means leads to failure in the
    practice.
But this most wonderful ear-whispered instruction
Offers a meditation on the path of means.
That's what I've realized,
This practice is good!

To this Milarepa advised, "Lotön, don't get hung on a fundamental basis, don't reject any avenue, don't fall into one 'right way.' Mind can't be distilled to one exclusive thing, it can't be explained by one exclusive example, it can't be described by one exclusive word. Once you've realized this, you can call it whatever you like."

Lotön went off to meditate in the mountains. He applied this instruction to his practice, studied to remove all doubts and meditated to remove all imputations. That's how he became a close son-disciple of Milarepa and was given the name Meditator Tön, the Snow Lion.

14

SONGS OF HAPPINESS

Namo guru!

THE JETSUN MILAREPA was staying at Upper Red Rock, near Drin, when a local teacher came up. Teacher Dre had never met Milarepa before, but he'd heard of him, felt inspired and wanted to see him.

Now here he was: and nothing in the cave except for a cooking pot. Dre thought, *No books, no shrine, no dharma things, not the slightest comfort . . . How'll he cope when he's dying?*

Milarepa had read his thoughts, "Teacher, don't worry! I've got the greatest books and the greatest shrine. I'm ready to die, I've got no regrets. Listen to my song." And he sang:

> Father Lamas, I pay my respects!
> My body is the mandala of a king
> My heart is filled with bliss deities past, present and future.
> With their blessings I'm not hung up on ownership.
> I make offerings day and night
> I'm happy without external possessions.
>
> The three realms of samsara are magical mansions
> All sentient beings have Buddha nature

With an instruction pointing out great awareness
Wherever I stay looks like a castle
Whomever I meet is a yidam deity
Whatever I do unfolds in the expanse of reality.
I'm happy without external shrines.

To the page red and white
I touch the ink of wisdom
And trace the five senses.
What shows up is dharma-body.
I'm happy without external texts.

Beings of the samsaric world
Already have the essence, but don't recognize it.
I practice with a profound oral instruction—
It's good, this samadhi of bodies inseparable.
At some point, I'll die. I'm fine with that.

So it's true! thought the teacher in a burst of devotion. *He can really read the minds of others. The rest must be true too.* From his heart he cried out, "Lama, please look after me!" Milarepa recognized him as a disciple with good karma, gave him empowerments and instructions, and sent him to meditate. Such blissful experiences arose!

The teacher went before the Jetsun (who had disciples around at the time) and said, "I never felt bliss like this in the days when I was holding on to my possessions. You, Jetsun, cling to nothing and enjoy bliss from within. Now I'm going to wander across the wilderness just like you and stay happy!"

This pleased the Jetsun who replied, "If you stay in solitary retreat, you'll always be happy! Later, you'll become an excellent guide on the path. Here's my Song on Eight Kinds of Happiness—"

And he sang:

Master, wish-fulfilling jewel, compassionate emanation,
Emperor behind the wheel, invaluable one,

Great lamp that dispels the darkness of ignorance,
At your feet, Marpa the translator, I bow down!

This mighty fortress—Upper Red Rock Cave—
Is a gathering spot for the four kinds of dakinis.
An old man like me gets such delight in this place
That I'm singing a song of happiness!
Hardy meditators, sitting for now
With your sharp minds: listen!

This particular spot in no particular place
Guides and guards one's meditation experience.
Has anyone tried it?
Your body's the monastery: happiness!
And your mind is clean as the sky.
Emaho! [46]

This strong, steady faith
Steers you away from samsara.
Has anyone tried it?
Samsara and nirvana are free in their own state: happiness!
In mind all dimensions are perfect.
Emaho!

This multifarious show of the six aggregates
Transforms bad conditions into the path.
Has anyone tried it?
Craving desire is exhausted: happiness!
Now cut the rope that binds perceiver and perceived.
Emaho!

This Lama with the transmission
Helps clear the darkness of ignorance.
Has anyone tried it?
Put stock in the Lama as the Buddha: happiness!

And mind will recognize its own face.
Emaho!

This bit of cotton knows no temperature
And guides my pilgrimage across the mountain range.
Has anyone tried it?
No more fretting about heat or cold: happiness!
Ah, to sleep naked in the snow.
Emaho!

This oral teaching on mixing and ejecting the consciousness
Frees me from fears of the bardo.
Has anyone tried it?
No split between this life and the next: happiness!
At last in the sphere of reality.
Emaho!

This ear-whispered lineage has a profound method
That clears the stains on mind's lucidity.
Has anyone tried it?
Bliss evermore for mind and body: happiness!
The life force surges in the central channel.
Emaho!

This yogi practices emptiness and compassion
And cuts through conventional constructs.
Has anyone tried it?
A circle of experienced beings: happiness!
Such a gathering of emanations.
Emaho!

This old-timer, inspired with joy,
Sings a song of experience on eight kinds of happiness
For you, here, now.
May it light up your practice.
Remember it! Keep it in your heart!

MILAREPA'S SONG DELIGHTED his disciples. "Wonderful!" exclaimed
Teacher Dre. "Now could you please tell us how to avoid errors in the
view, meditation, conduct and fruition—keeping it simple for us . . ?"

"Well," replied Milarepa, "here's how you should practice." And
he sang the Song of Avoiding Errors:

> Father Lamas, I pay homage!
> If you want to get the point about the view,
> Don't stain the wisdom of consciousness with study.
> Until you've truly realized the natural state,
> Don't spill words about emptiness.
> All that manifests is like an echo
> Bouncing back in good or harm.
> So think of cause and effect, and don't kill!
> Until you've truly realized the tantric approach,
> Don't get caught up in *words* about *mind,*
> Holding too tight to your views.
> Don't criticize others!
>
> If you want to practice meditation,
> Dispel the doubts within, letting the natural state manifest.
> Until the clear light of mind shines,
> Don't get attached to your experiences
> And don't grasp at some solid fort of emptiness.
> Perceptions are appearance-emptiness united,
> So let desires subside of themselves.
> It's all empty of true nature
> But don't get hung up on emptiness.
> Don't be forming definitions!
> In this world, waves of pleasure
> Can make vulgar concepts subside.
> But don't think you're tasting bliss!
> During steady, concept-free calm abiding,
> Don't cling to holiness.

If you want to savor the one flavor of all modes of conduct:
Until experiences and realizations arise within,
Don't start giving blessings.
Until the bliss of the five senses arises
And conceptual constructs come to an end,
Don't pervert the yogas
Or push others to practice "union and liberation."

If you want to actualize fruition:
Until you've seen the face of your own mind,
Don't search for enlightenment elsewhere
And don't work yourself into a tizzy with hopes and fears!
Your disciples may perceive you as an emanation,
But don't think you're the Buddha in person!

Even if your conceptual thoughts dissolve into the dharma-
    body,
Don't get stuck on the notion that what once existed has
    now ceased.
Qualities, enlightened activity, pure realms—
These are the natural manifestation of pristine awareness.
Don't look outside for them.

TEACHER DRE GAINED conviction. He spent a long time meditating in
solitude. Special signs of experience—such as inner heat—appeared.
He took the name Good Luck Blaze and became a close disciple of
Milarepa.

15

To a woman

Namo guru!

THE WOMAN LEKSEBUM said to Milarepa, "Why don't you stay at my place for a while?" and she extended the invitation to his student, Rechungpa. She knew the Jetsun never did stay anywhere for long; indeed, a week later, he would be gone.

One night, while Milarepa was there, she said she wanted to go to a party in town. "They're making *tsatsas*,"[47] she explained, "it'll be fun. Are you coming?"

"No, thanks," replied Milarepa.

"But today is so auspicious!" said Leksebum, who'd already dressed up. "At least make an offering in my shrine. You can make tsatsas there if you want."

And so saying, she headed for the door, listing chores for Milarepa: make sure the baby is all right, look after the sheep, keep an eye on the place, thanks.

That evening, Milarepa and his student were deep in meditation— even as the sheep grazed the grass, even as the baby screamed. When Leksebum returned, she was mad. "I can see why you wouldn't do the household work," she started, "but you're Buddhists! How can you just sit with a baby and sheep out of control? Maybe you think that's kind?"

In response, Milarepa sang this Song of Experience:

> I was guarding the sheep of changeless nature
> In the meadow of great bliss.
> There was no chance to guard sheep of flesh and blood.
> You, Leksebum, do that.

> I was caring for the child of awareness
> With the love and compassion of a mother.
> There was no chance to care for a sniffling baby.
> You, Leksebum, do that.

> I was making tsatsas of undistracted mindfulness
> On the mountain of unwavering meditation.
> There was no chance to make clay tsatsas.
> You, Leksebum, do that.

> I was offering lamps of meditation
> At the shrine of emptiness.
> There was no chance to offer oil lamps.
> You, Leksebum, do that.

> I was scrubbing the habitual patterns
> From my unreal decaying body.
> There was no chance to scrub your house.
> You, Leksebum, do that.

> I was polishing my game of illusions
> With the appearances of the world.
> There was no chance to polish your dishes.
> You, Leksebum, do that.

SHE SAID, "Don't put me down just because my activities aren't as lofty as yours." She stopped and then added, "I've served other Lamas too, you know."

Milarepa responded with a Song about Activities:

> Serving a Lama without compassion
> Is like serving a child-eating demon!
>
> Practicing dharma without bodhichitta
> Is like a fool playing tricks on himself:
> You stir your own passions.
>
> Making gifts based on prejudice
> Is like feeding a glutton:[48]
> You enlarge your own hopes.
>
> Making inappropriate offerings
> Is like giving to a con man:
> You only make things more confused.
>
> Giving without affection
> Is like tying yourself to a pillar:
> You only bind yourself.
>
> Having no control over your own mind
> Is like a show-off forever bragging:
> You lose sight of cause and effect.
>
> Meditating without a pith instruction
> Is like a trickster conjuring a house:
> You're the one to get exposed.
>
> Tantric practice without the right connection
> Is like a madman drinking hot water:
> You only feel more thirsty.
>
> If your activities haven't been that lofty,
> You've wrapped yourself in damaged silk:

Inside, the rot is spreading.

If the fruit of your practice is still self-absorbed,
You've formed something out of clay:
One blow, it's in pieces.

THIS HIT LEKSEBUM. She apologized to Milarepa and fished a turquoise
stone from her jewelry box. "Please teach me!" she said, placing the
gem in his hands.
   So Milarepa sang her this Vajra Song:

   Listen, Leksebum, rich lady,
   You're an intelligent woman.

   Take a good look at your body:
   Meditate without lusting.

   Take a good look at your words:
   Meditate without verbalizing.

   Take a good look at your mind:
   Meditate without conceptualizing.

   Keep in line your body and your words and your mind.
   Meditate without meditating.

SHE WENT OFF to meditate. There were experiences, and she sang a
song for Milarepa:

   You marvelous yogi clad in cotton
   With the audacious mind
   You, man of no fear
   Man of no bond
   You ascetic, you yogi:

To you, I give my respect
To you, I make this offering
To you I say: I'm sorry for my mistakes.
You delight me, teacher.
Please teach the dharma
Please don't leave for nirvana.
I dedicate merit to all sentient beings.

I've looked at my own body
And tried to meditate without lusting.
But the lust is still there.

I've looked at my own words
And tried to meditate without verbalizing.
But the words are still there.

I've looked at my own mind
And tried to meditate without conceptualizing.
But the concepts are still there.

I've tried to keep in line my body, my words and my mind,
Tried to meditate without meditating,
But "meditation" is still there.

Please clear this up, help me out!

So THE JETSUN sang this Song to Leksebum:

Listen, Leksebum!

If you crave physical pleasure,
Stop socializing, get away from people
And give away everything you have.
Then relax in a state of no attachment.

If you're verbalizing, formulating,
Turn your back on petty concerns
And watch your pride, your self-aggrandizement,
Then relax in a state of no vanity.

If your mind is full of concepts,
Anchor it with the iron hook of mindfulness
And don't take samsara and nirvana as two.
Then relax in a state of equanimity.

Relax without chasing the thoughts that come up.
If you still find yourself fixated on meditating,
Then meditate with affection for all sentient beings
Meditate that your body, your words, your mind, are all great
   compassion
Meditate that the Lama sits on top of your head
Meditate at length on emptiness.
At the end, dedicate the merit.

Think about this, practice the sublime dharma.

LEKSEBUM PRACTICED ACCORDING to Milarepa's advice and became a
yogini on the path.

16

TO MY STUDENT

Namo guru!

THE JETSUN MILAREPA was staying at Tiny Cave with his students. Two of them, Rechungpa and Drigom Repa, were in a heated discussion about the teachings of Maitripa[49] and Naropa when the Jetsun Milarepa interrupted, "You two, listen to my song, then go on with your debate!" And he sang the Song of Cutting Through Misperceptions:

> On the crown of my head is the kind Lama
> Giving me such joy, I feel happy!
> A sense of inseparability has arisen in me.
>
> You two—acting out or meditating in the world of action—
> If you haven't got it from the inside
> You're nothing but arrogant blabbering mouths!
>
> You're better off cutting the imputations from within.
> Isn't it called the view free of extremes?
> Enhance it then with textual references and logic.

As for conceptual thoughts subsiding in the dharma-body,
Don't we talk of self-arising meditation?
You've got to expand it with experiences and realizations.

Then there's the six senses that are pure in themselves,
Which, correct me if I'm wrong, is about savoring the one
    taste.
It's all about timing, you'll get this right.

When the experience of bliss-emptiness arises,
We call it the ear-whispered transmission—don't we?
How about dressing this up in the four empowerments?

When the visionary experience of emptiness opens up,
Don't we refer to a gradual path proceeding in stages?
Make it beautiful with signs along the way.

And the cessation of mind when it rests in its own state—
That's Buddhahood in a single lifetime, right?
Why not embroider it with the four bodies?

If someone has textual logic and the oral instruction,
Isn't that a Lama with a transmission?
The adornment of compassion gives it beauty.

A good heart together with pure faith
Make for a suitable student, wouldn't you say?
Enrich it then with respect and commitment.

The view makes mind clear to you
Meditation engages you in practice
And conduct upholds you to the end.
The results show in the mind:
You realize all things as one.

THIS CUT THROUGH misperceptions on both sides. Milarepa continued,
"Rechungpa, if you're sincere about practicing—" And he sang, Are
You Confident:

> Child, awareness-holder, listen now!
> To practice the dharma, here's what you need:
>
> The Lama is the Buddha of all times
> He's developed all qualities:
> In truth he's dharma-body.
> Are you confident, or still uncertain?
>
> From his mouth the oral instructions spill
> Like magic pills to remove the five poisons:
> In truth they're nectar.
> Are you confident, or still wavering?
>
> What he does is free
> Enlightened activity:
> In truth it's emanation body.
> Are you confident, or still hesitant?
>
> Fireworks of frenzied thoughts in the mind
> Explode—yet they never arose, never had a basis.
> What you want is imperturbable mindfulness.
> Are you convinced, or still not sure?
>
> Nauseous waves of neurotic emotions
> Cause deep ravage, like a tree burnt at the root.
> Never be bound!
> Are you convinced, or still not clear?
>
> In the realm of desire you find the pleasures of the gods
> But like the four seasons, they pass.
> There's no final happiness in samsara.
> Are you convinced, or still uncertain?

All phenomena, all composite things
Are as impermanent as a flash of lightning across the sky,
Drops in a stream, the smoke of incense.
Not much leisure in this life.
Are you convinced, or still thinking about it?

One thing for sure is death for you, death for everyone.
No one can escape it!
What you need is accomplishment beyond death.
Are you convinced now, or still not quite?

ONE AND ALL, the students felt a new and greater confidence.

ONE DAY, LOCALS from nearby Nyanang invited Rechungpa for a feast offering. Milarepa agreed he could go there for two weeks and Rechungpa departed along with other students who were on their way to seek alms.

So when a group of patrons and villagers—Dzese, Kochuk etc.—came to see the Jetsun, they found him stark naked. They were deeply embarrassed and couldn't bring themselves to get closer. Finally Dzese picked up a sheet and rushed to cover Milarepa.

"Jetsun," he started, "you've got to understand, we're regular people, it's so . . . you know, it's just so uncomfortable when you're naked like that. Please, I'm asking you, cover yourself with this sheet."

Milarepa stood up all at once, completely naked, and sang the Shameless Song:

I've walked and walked so many places,
I can't remember my homeland.

I've stayed and stayed with my Lama
And can't remember my family.

I've cherished and cherished the meaning of pure dharma
And can't remember the worldly dharma.

I've wandered and wandered all alone
And can't remember about agitation.

I've looked and looked at monkeys play
And can't remember about cattle and sheep.

I've used and used a tinder pouch
And can't remember about home accessories.

I've lived as neither a master nor a servant
And forgot about social artifice.

I've been free, free, free
And forgot about shame.

I've dealt with my mind
And forgot about covering up.

I've sparked inner heat in my body
And forgot about clothes.

I've meditated on non-conceptual wisdom
And forgot conceptual thought.

I've meditated on the clear-light nature of reality
And forgot mental constructs.

These twelve forgotten things
Are the teachings of a yogi.
Why don't you do the same?

I'm free of the shackles of duality,
Why should I conform?

Not for me the fabricated.
For me enlightenment.

How difficult your regular dharma is.
Me I'm free, I'm carefree
While you talk of shame, you hypocrites!
But I don't know how to pretend.

THE VILLAGERS SAID nothing but they made their offerings and then
left. As for Rechungpa down in the village, he only stayed one night
at each person's place, but still it was a long time before he made it
back to the Jetsun. When he finally returned, the entrance to the cave
was all sealed. *He must be displeased because I was gone so long,* thought
Rechungpa. So he sang:

The natural state is without provisions.
Saving provisions—that's not the natural state.

The great perfection is without a preferred direction.
A preferred direction—that's not the great perfection.

Mahamudra is without stopping or going.
Stopping or going—that's not Mahamudra.

Great bliss is without light or shadow.
Light or shadow—that's not great bliss.

The middle way is without identification.
Identification—that's not the middle way.

I, Rechungpa, have just returned.
Father Jetsun, how are you?

FROM THE TOP of the door came Milarepa's voice:

There's no Buddha outside your mind
No faster path than the energy flowing through the channels
   of your body

No better friend than the refuge of Buddha, dharma, sangha
No finer experience than bliss-emptiness
No greater kindness than your Lama
On the crown of all beings.

If you practice without error
You'll definitely understand.

If you feel you've explored every avenue
You'll find the oral instructions a resource.

If you're clear about your own mind
You'll be resolute, and signs will appear.

If you develop kindness in your heart
You'll learn to feel compassion for all beings.

If you see your Lama as the Buddha
You'll be infused with waves of blessing.

Your verses were excellent.
If you actually *get* what you said,
You're on the right track.
Otherwise, it's just hot air.

How are you, Rechungpa, my child?
Your old father is doing well.

AFTER THIS SONG, Milarepa brought down the wall of rocks that had sealed his cave.

"Come in, come in!" he said and then, taking a look at his student, he laughed, "Hmm! You're still attached to the world out there, aren't you? You need to learn to meditate in solitude." And he sang the Song of Solitary Practice:

Father Lama, your blessings have put me here,
Pray keep me on the mountain.
Rechungpa, my fortunate student,
Listen carefully!

When you're set in a solitary spot,
Don't think back to family stuff
Or dark feelings will arise.

When you're meditating by the Lama,
Don't be busy trying to add up
Or you'll be at war—evil deeds are legion.

When you make offerings to the elemental spirits,
Don't even think of piling them up
Or you'll become a spirit yourself.

When you're in meditation retreat,
Don't be socializing
Or your good practice will be weakened.

When you lead the hard life of an ascetic,
Don't fantasize about food
Or you'll be reborn a hungry ghost.

When you practice the skillful path that's been ear-whispered,
Don't think about intellectual studies
Or you'll get on the wrong track.

When you're all alone on the mountain,
Don't be itching to go
Or you'll get in a bad mood.

Child, to advance on the path you need stamina,
To reject samsara's misery you need hardship.

Child, you're connected to me by good merit,
May realizations dawn!
All that comes up and all that goes on is dharma-body—
May this experience bloom in you.

THE SONG CUT RAW to the bone. In reply, Rechungpa prostrated and
sang this song:

Father Lama, your kindness led me to the dharma.
I turned my back on my gentle parents
And left behind my homeland. It was hard.
Sometimes I just want to be around others.

It's not that I'm trying to hoard food, clothes or money,
I'm not really mean or greedy by nature.
But asceticism and hard practice in a cave—
Sometimes I just think about having things.

You're an adept, I know, I know.
I've got the ear-whispered transmission
And do I ever meditate—and how!
Sometimes I just want to meet another teacher.

I've been at your feet
Practicing for enlightenment in a single life,
Living alone in the mountains like a hermit.
Sometimes I just want to do things.

Jetsun, unchangeable essence, Vajradhara,
Please help me change!

THE JETSUN MILAREPA gave Rechungpa pith instructions. Rechungpa
took these to heart and greatly improved. Afterwards, they were both
invited by locals from Nyanang to stay at Belly Cave.

17

TWO MAD YOGIS

Namo guru!

AT BELLY CAVE IN NYANANG, Milarepa saw the Lion-Face Dakini as the sun was rising. "Milarepa," she said, "the Indian Dampa Sangye[50] is going to Tongla. Won't you go see him?"

Milarepa thought, *I don't need clarification on anything, but he's a great adept, I see no harm in meeting him.* He held his breath and cut through space. An instant later, he was in the valley near Tongla. Seeing a group of traders, he called out to them, "Do you know if Dampa Sangye has arrived? He's from India."

"Dampa Sangye? Doesn't sound familiar. But an old teacher with a face wrinkled and blue slept at the inn last night."

That must be him, the traders just didn't recognize him, decided Milarepa. He walked up the mountain pass and saw Dampa Sangye. The latter had also been urged by the Lion-Face Dakini to go meet the Jetsun, and after a night at The Responsive Inn, he was doing just that.

Well now, mused Milarepa as they saw each other in the distance, *they all say that Dampa Sangye has supernatural powers. Let's test him!*

He transformed himself into a patch of bright flowers and saw Dampa Sangye walk right by him. But just as Milarepa was beginning to wonder, Dampa Sangye turned around and pushed his foot amid the flowers, saying to himself, *These flowers are Milarepa, I probably shouldn't put my foot there.* And then addressing the patch of color in the grass, "You sing the heart-songs of the dakinis. Carnivorous as they are, though, they're mad at you, and they're draining your life force. They've taken your heart, they even celebrated last night—I know, I saw them eat your heart. Your last breath is tonight, then you are no more. Doesn't death make you uncomfortable?"

All at once the Jetsun sprung up and sang the Song of Six-Fold Trust in the Face of Death:

> The lion of no extremes
> Has no fear, bares his fangs
> And sleeps easy in the snow.
> I'm a yogi, I trust this view.
> I understand it, so for me,
> Death is part of the path to liberation.
>
> The stag that stands still
> Has elaborate horns of one-taste
> And rests in the meadow of clear bliss.
> I'm a yogi, I trust this meditation.
> I understand it, so for me,
> Death is part of the path to liberation.
>
> The fish of ten virtues
> Has rolling golden eyes
> And flows the stream of continual experience.
> I'm a yogi, I trust this conduct.
> I understand it, so for me,
> Death is part of the path to liberation.
>
> The rising tigress of mind
> Has stripes of consideration
> And roams the vast forests.
> I'm a yogi, I trust this commitment.

I understand samaya, so for me,
Death is part of the path to liberation.

On the paper red and white,
I write letters of awareness
And watch them spell non-duality.
I'm a yogi, I trust this holy dharma.
I understand it, so for me,
Death is part of the path to liberation.

The eagle of mind, whose flight is smooth,
Has wings of merit and wisdom
And scythes the sky that never was.
I'm a yogi, I trust this result.
I understand fruition, so for me,
Death is part of the path to liberation.

"YOU MAKE NO SENSE at all!" replied Dampa Sangye. "How can you use external things as examples? If you were a real yogi, you would cut to the core of immediate experience."

So Milarepa burst into the Song of Six-Fold Bliss:

In the remote reaches that dakinis favor,
I alone dwell, relaxed, engaged in the pure dharma.

I salute the annihilation of ego
And my mind, beyond birth,
Reaches that which is beyond death.
Coming into, going out—these notions are set free.
I'm clear about the view, my mind is at ease.
Bliss, this practice!

In the meditation of non-meditation,
I pulse in perfect concentration.
Meditation, post-meditation—these ideas are set free.

I'm clear about meditation, my mind is at ease.
Bliss, this practice!

I move unencumbered
In the sphere of spontaneous conduct
As claims of right and wrong are set free.
I'm clear about conduct, my mind is at ease.
Bliss, this practice!

I stir without attainment
In a state of no empowerment
As concepts of deity-body are set free.
I'm clear about empowerment, my mind is at ease.
Bliss, this practice!

I proceed without fault
Where there are no commitments.
Notions of vows to keep are set free.
I understand samaya, my mind is at ease.
Bliss, this practice!

In the land of no result,
I have no expectations.
Hopes and fears—these notions are set free.
I understand fruition, my mind is at ease.
Bliss, this practice!

"Now that," said Dampa Sangye, "is something I have also experienced. At last Tibet has a yogi who needs no further tutoring! Mind you, your type is hard to find even in India." And in a gracious tone, he added, "You and I are past needing one another, it appears."

Already Dampa Sangye was turning around, but the Jetsun caught his robe and said, "Dampa! I've heard that you have a teaching called the *Pacifying*, it's supposed to ease all suffering. I'm told that by shifting one's mind in meditation, it's possible to attain enlightenment all at once. Please sing me a song about it."

"No one's heard me sing about it before, and no one will hear me sing about it now."

But as the Jetsun insisted, Dampa finally sang the Song that Eases Suffering:

> When demons assail you,
> It's time to turn ascetic and do yoga.
> When your body withers,
> It's time to fuse your mind with space.
> When subtle concepts arise,
> It's time to first stir and then transcend your passions.
> When you lie down by your secret self,
> It's time to lay bare your awareness.
> When you're in crowds,
> It's time to face appearances.
> When you feel lethargic,
> It's time to jolt yourself by shouting PHET![51]
> When you feel scattered,
> It's time to center yourself.
> When you're agitated,
> It's time to open up to space.
>
> This teaching turns all difficulties
> Into valuable challenges.
> It's a holy teaching that eases suffering
> It's the aim of the Buddhas past, present and future
> The secret word of Vajradhara
> The secret heart of the dakinis
> The pith of the four classes of tantra[52]
> The ear-whispered transmission
> The key to oral instructions
> The teaching of the *Pacifying*.

THE JETSUN LISTENED to Dampa Sangye with keen pleasure. Absorbed
in the song, he'd been sitting with his penis freely exposed. Dampa
Sangye now exclaimed, "Look at you! That's the one place you really
should keep covered up . . . I wonder if you're not a bit mad." So the
Jetsun sang the Song of the Madman:

> Homage to the holy Lamas!
> I take refuge in your kindness.
> Please dispel obstacles
> And lead me the right way.
>
> People ask themselves,
> Isn't Milarepa a bit mad?
> In truth, I think I am,
> And here's the method to my madness:
>
> Mad father, mad son—
> Madness is passed on.
> Great Vajradhara is mad,
> My ancestor, the excellent Tilopa, is quite mad,
> And my grandfather, Naropa, is definitely mad.
> Mad is my old father Marpa,
> And I, Milarepa, why, I'm mad too!
> This Vajradhara transmission
> Of four enlightened bodies is madness.
> Tilopa's Mahamudra
> Is an absolute madness.
> Naropa's ascetic awareness
> Is mad, mad, mad!
> My father, Marpa Lotsawa,
> Is crazed by the demons of the four classes of tantra.
> I, Milarepa, know mind and energy—
> Most certainly a madness.
>
> Mad is the view that holds no favorite
> Mad the meditation that refuses references

Mad the conduct that hides no agenda
Mad the result that preys on neither hopes nor fears
Mad the promises kept honestly.

I'm more than mad, I'm a raving lunatic—
I drive demons mad
With the Lamas' instructions.
I turn witches mad
With the dakinis' blessings.
I dement the happy demented
With ultimate absorption.
I craze she-demons of realization
With games of enjoyment.

I'm more than a raving lunatic, I'm really sick—
I've got backaches from Mahamudra
And chest pains from Dzogchen
I'm weak from "vase breathing"
Feverish with wisdom from above
Chilled by meditation from below
Hot and cold from bliss and emptiness.
I vomit—ugh! There's the oral instructions.
Then reality arouses me, and I lie back.

I'm beyond sickness, I'm a dead man—
In the view, which is vast,
I died along with my prejudices.
In meditation, which is spacious,
I died along with my ups and downs.
In conduct, which is extensive,
I died along with my moral claims.
In fruition, which is inclusive
I died along with my hopes and fears.
In samaya, which is universal,
I died along with my pretenses.

I, the yogi, died
In the planes of enlightenment.

I'm to die tonight? No shrouds for my body then:
Rather, the subtle perceptions of external appearances.
No strings for me:
Rather, the rope of the central channel.
No maudlin relatives:
Rather, the child-disciple of awareness.
For this yogi's body, no gray funeral:
Rather, the path to enlightenment.

Guided by the dakinis,
Led by the Kagyu Lamas—
No meadow on a hill for my corpse:
Rather, the peak of Samantabhadra.
No cemeteries visited by foxes:
Rather, the pleasure grounds of wisdom and skillful means.
Yes! Vajradhara's own grave!

DAMPA SANGYE WAS tickled. "I get your kind of madness!" he grinned.

"What would you say if we performed a feast offering?" Milarepa responded.

"You're the host here," said Dampa Sangye, "why don't you set it up?"

So Milarepa split his own skull and took out his brains. He chopped off his neck and both his legs—these served to form the fire pit. Next he blazed flames from the tummo inner heat at his navel, setting his skull on fire brightly. Now Dampa Sangye turned his body into seven replicas, each sitting on a stalk of grass. Milarepa transformed into seven mandalas of the deity Demchok, complete with eight gates, and settled on seven grass stalks as well, sated with feast offerings. But the seven sprigs had bent a little under the transfigured Milarepa, whereas they stood straight under Dampa Sangye. The Jetsun asked

Dampa why that might be, since they both appeared equally proficient in their "vase breathing" techniques.

"It must be because you're Tibetan!" replied Dampa Sangye. "But as for the view and the practice, we're on the exact same wavelength. Your realization and mine are the same. Our future disciples will see eye to eye."

AFTER A TIME, Dampa Sangye and Milarepa used their magical powers to return each to his own home.

18

BUBBLES BORNE AWAY

Namo guru!

MILAREPA AND HIS STUDENTS were on their way to Tongla when five robbers pounced on them. But there wasn't much to steal: a search of three of Milarepa's five disciples yielded only a few skulls. At this point the robbers asked, "You guys are 'The Milarepas,' right?"

"Well, I am Milarepa," said the Jetsun.

"Oh, we've scored big!" said one of the robbers as they all prostrated. "Please teach us the dharma."

Milarepa gave them a teaching on cause and effect, the results of good or bad deeds, the advantages of a higher rebirth and the many problems with rebirth in the lower realms. To conclude, he sang them a Song about What's Worth Pursuing and What's Better Avoided:

At the feet of the genuine Lama, I bow!

In the joyful heaven,
The gods sow rice and it grows well.
There's nothing unique about their farming,
It's just karma—they're reaping merit of old.
Good robbers, don't be greedy!

In the eighteen hells,
The doomed are stabbed and healed, and stabbed and healed.
There's nothing unique about their skin,
It's just karma—they're paying for past murders.
Good robbers, don't kill!

In the desolate land of spirits,
Ghosts eat and eat but can't ease their hunger.
There's nothing unique about their bellies,
It's just karma—they're eating back their jealousy.
Good robbers, don't be envious!

By the mythical Wash Pond
Stands the bountiful cow.
Will you milk her? It's up to you.

Under the magical tree
Grows the cure-all miracle herb.
Will you dig for it? It's up to you.

In the presence of a guru with his students
Shines the key of the oral transmission.
Will you unlock the door to merit and wisdom? It's up to
you.

THE ROBBERS WERE greatly inspired. Four of them vowed there and then never to kill or rob again. The fifth one decided to go with Milarepa and gained excellent realizations.

AFTER THIS ENCOUNTER, the Jetsun and his students went to Dingri Mar. They met a shepherd and Milarepa asked him who the local patron was. He was advised to try Doctor Yange, said to be rich and devoted. Milarepa with disciples headed for the doctor's place.

Once there, Milarepa made his way through the many people mill-
ing about and approached Doctor Yange. "We're told you're a rich
patron," he said by way of introduction. "We'd appreciate some food."

"Do you yogis ever stop? Already there's Milarepa on the other
side of the mountain, and Dampa Sangye on this side. I can't give to
every yogi, you know. Milarepa, that's different, I'd give to him any
day if he came here. But I don't expect to be that lucky."

"Actually, I am Milarepa. Now, about the food?"

"You're Milarepa! I'm told you can turn anything into a dharma
teaching. See the bubbles in the ditch here? Please use them to sing a
dharma song." So the Jetsun sang the Song of Bubbles Borne Away:

> I bow at the feet of my Lama, forever the Buddha.
> May all appearances point to the dharma.
>
> My Lama said that life is like a bubble borne away:
> Nothing is solid, nothing is certain.
>
> Sloth is like a thief in an empty house:
> You come out empty-handed. Maybe you knew that?
>
> Youth is like a summer bloom:
> It's passed before you know it.
>
> Old age is like a forest fire:
> Suddenly it's caught up with you. Maybe you knew that?
>
> Birth and death are like sunrise, sunset:
> Now here, now gone. So the Buddha said.
>
> Illness is like a bird hit by a stone:
> Getting weaker and weaker. Maybe you knew that?
>
> Death is like the last flicker of light:
> Nothing lasts forever.

Bad karma is like a waterfall:
It only ever goes down. Maybe you knew that?

The damned are like poison:
Touch them and you'll turn rank.

Breaking your word is like beans after a freeze:
There's rot, and it spreads.

Dharma practitioners are like farmers:
With care, they succeed.

The Lama is like medicine:
Rely on him and you'll be fine.

Your samaya vow is like a watchtower:
Guard it and you'll get ahead.

Cause and effect are like the wheel of life:
Too much carelessness will cost you.

Samsara is like a poisonous thorn:
The prick only gets worse.

The Lord of Death is like shadows at sunset:
It's harder and harder to see.

When your time is up
Where will you find refuge
If not in the holy dharma?
Dharma leads to victory
But does anyone really try?

Samsaric creatures are born in misery
Miserably, they compete and plunder.

Then there are those who love to talk about the dharma,
But dare them with the real stuff, and it's another story.

Patron, don't talk too much,
Better you practice the dharma.

"AN EXCELLENT SONG, very helpful," declared Doctor Yange. "Would
you please give a teaching on birth, old age, sickness and death, and
on karma? I'd like to be clearer on this."

In response, Milarepa sang the Song of Old Age, Sickness and
Death:

In the reality of no arising,
Lama, you spill nectar—
Nectar of love, compassion, joy, equanimity.
You've laid out the way to bliss,
You're a wish-fulfilling jewel. Homage to you!

Listen to my words, patron, listen to my praise, people.

You're young, fresh and strong
You don't really think about old age.
But it creeps in, more so every day—
A seed, a sprout, then full-blown.

You're fit, vibrant and active
You don't really think about illness.
But it hits you all at once—
It shakes and shatters and smashes you.

You're busy, working, up-and-doing
You don't really think about death.
But one day it scythes you down—
Startling sudden lightning.

Old age, illness, death—
What a familiar refrain.
When troubles come,
The Lord of Death lurks
And springs his trap on you.
Life, and death, and in-between,
They trail each other
Like birds in the sky
Never far from you.

How's that still, small voice? You're afraid?

Life in the netherworld—
The hellish, brutish, disembodied netherworld—
Is just around the corner, waiting in ambush.
But for a narrow defile,
There's no exit.

How are the skeletons in your closet? Bothering you?

Suffering is like a rock sending ripples in the water,
If you don't deal with it, it expands.
If you don't free yourself,
Joy brushes you, then sorrow scrapes you—
The passers-by of life.
You just see their face, already they've passed.
Be conscious of impermanence:
You're basking in the summer sun
Then, before you know it,
Living through a blizzard.
Practice the dharma!

HEARING THIS SONG, the various house guests joined the doctor in
expressing their respect and admiration for Milarepa. They presented

him with offerings and the doctor invited Milarepa to stay for good.
But the Jetsun declined: he would stay only for the night.

Next morning, Doctor Yange asked for oral instructions and gathered the villagers for the teaching, saying, "Jetsun, you won't be here
more than a day, please teach us how to practice."

Milarepa responded with a song on How to Practice:

> Listen my friends, and ask yourselves,
> Do you really want to practice?
> If you do, then try this:
>
> When you lie down, don't let crass ignorance lull you to
>   sleep
> At dusk, practice your yidam deity
> Then pray to your Lama
> And at midnight, meditate without concepts
> In the small hours of the night, focus on your energies
> At dawn, acknowledge your errors
> And as the sun rises, take on appearances.
>
> Ask your Lama for oral instructions,
> Pray to your yidam deity
> Keep your word to your vajra brothers and sisters
> Make offerings to the three gems—Buddha, dharma, sangha
> Visualize Chenrezig[53] on your head
> And recite his mantra—*Om Mani Pedme Hung.*
>
> Give to those who have less
> Be generous in spirit and in practice
> Give your support to scholars
> And respect your parents.
>
> You could have a hundred Lamas here,
> They wouldn't give you better advice.

May it go well for you!
A long and healthy life to you all!

IT'S NO EXAGGERATION to say that the crowd at Doctor Yange's was swept with devotion. The doctor himself entered the path of dharma on his deathbed.

Now Jetsun Milarepa and his disciples left Dingri Mar and went towards Chubar.

19

SEPARATION

Namo guru!

THERE WAS A SLIGHT PROBLEM with Rechungpa and it had to do with a woman.

Milarepa knew he'd have to clear this up, so he metamorphosed into a beggar and came to Rechungpa. "Give me alms!" he asked. Rechungpa took out a turquoise gem (it came from Yakder Valley) and gave it to the beggar, saying, "This should get you some food."

Well, my son isn't greedy, thought Milarepa, *he's got a kind heart.*

Let's just say that Rechungpa giving away the turquoise was one of the factors in his breakup with Dembu—that was her name. They fought, he left. He was walking back to the Jetsun now. He was walking and he met a woman, whose father was rich, who gave him two slabs of dried meat. These he kept as a gift for Milarepa.

At this same moment, Milarepa was in Chubar and announced to the disciples around him, "Ah, Rechungpa has a present, it's so huge it won't fit into the valley." Almost at once, Rechungpa showed up, offered a slab of dried meat to Milarepa and asked him if he was well.

In response, the Jetsun sang the song, Sure I'm Well:

I'm a yogi who roams the snows.
Bliss expands: a mandala.
No toxics here, no sickness,
Sure I'm well.

Alone, I power myself.
No escape, no distractions,
Sure I'm well.

I've got no errands to run.
No-man's land, nothing to do,
Sure I'm well.

I don't do home ownership.
No new toys, no need to shop,
Sure I'm well.

I don't need my words in print.
No concerns, nothing but mind,
Sure I'm well.

I don't say much—that makes you vain.
No small talk, no running on,
Sure I'm well.

I'm no faker playing games.
No designs, no strategies,
Sure I'm well.

I'm not really ambitious.
No cheap shots, no mud-slinging,
Sure I'm well.

I don't chose places or clothes.
No picking, no co-opting,
Sure I'm well.

I accept all that feeds me.
A man like me, sure I'm well.

And you, my son, Rechungpa,
How was your trip?

RECHUNGPA TOOK OUT the second slab of meat and shared it among the monks. One of them looked at Milarepa. "Jetsun," he said, "I thought Rechungpa's present was supposed to be too big to fill the valley. But I don't see anything like that."

"Don't you? Tell me now that this meat isn't too big for the valley between your ribs!"

As the laughter died down, Milarepa said, "All right, now I'm going to initiate all of you with an empowerment. You need to make an offering, it will set up a good connection for this ceremony. But you, Rechungpa," he continued, turning to his disciple, "don't bother."

Rechungpa was hurt and bewildered, but he went along anyway. Then he looked down at the very center of the mandala and saw the turquoise he'd given away. What? Further confusion until at last he figured out that the beggar to whom he'd given the turquoise must have been Milarepa. In his wisdom and kindness, Milarepa had done that to break off his relationship with Dembu. That had to be it.

"You know that turquoise would have brought you grief," Milarepa told him. "But your faith in me is strong and constant, and your compassion for others is great. They're your saving grace." And the Jetsun sang this song:

My Lama's grace is great
Milarepa's magic is great
Rechungpa's kindness is great.
Here's the turquoise you gave to a beggar,
Tonight, let's give it to Chakrasamvara.
An open heart and an open hand—
That's as good as an offering to the Buddhas.

Think about this: next time you give to a beggar
You'll be giving to Milarepa!

Everyone's been your parent in a previous life.
Why try and rank them? It's poison.

True scholars help each other.
Don't promote one school over another, it's a waste.

There's no good or evil in the dharma.
Spare the dharma your parochialism, it's death.

Your happiness is due to others,
Be good to them, you'll benefit too.
But hurt them, you'll mostly hurt yourself.
Arouse bodhichitta mind
Enter this divine mandala
Face your flaws
And keep your promises.

RECHUNGPA FELT FULL of regrets. He spilled his heart to Milarepa and
his dharma friends in this song:

I wanted physical pleasure, I admit
I went chasing after looks
I did all kinds of dirty things.
Now, Lama, you're here in the flesh,
I lay myself bare with all my flaws.

I had the gift of gab, I admit
It's the road to hell, but I was shameless
I was an animal, I guzzled, I swallowed.
Now, Lama, you're here, you sing,
I tell you how it was, I tell you all my flaws.

I wanted recognition, I admit
I did unsavory deals, I was nasty
It was pure self-interest.
Now, Lama, you're here, you know,
I unburden myself of all my flaws.

I stayed in towns bad and busy, I admit
It cost me my dharma friends, it cost me my practice
I did black magic, my mantras lost their power.
I was so active, my meditation faded.
Before this divine mandala, I face my flaws.

I stayed in a fussy house, I admit
I marked what was mine, what was others'
I wasn't noble enough to think
They were like my mother, my father.
Before my dharma friends, I confess my flaws.

AT THAT POINT, the Jetsun proceeded with the empowerment and gave a detailed teaching to point out the nature of mind. When it was over, the student Repa Zhiwa Ö waited until the others had left, then he approached Milarepa.

"Jetsun," he said, "Rechungpa's had many empowerments. He's mastered the practices that deal with mind and the energies of the body. What's so bad about him taking a secret consort? Is your permission required for that? And does he really have to lay out this stuff in front of everyone?"

"Oh, it's just a question of timing," replied Milarepa. "The conditions must be right." And he sang this Song about Timing:

At your feet, kind Marpa, I bow down!
Grant your blessings that I may advance on the path.
Help me understand the minds of my students.
Yogis are foolish if they don't practice at the right time

Old men are foolish if they don't speak at the right time
Mothers are foolish if they don't feed at the right time
Servants are foolish if they don't work at the right time
Heroes are foolish if they're not bold at the right time
Monks are foolish if they don't persevere at the right time
Pure hearts are foolish if they don't renounce at the right
time.

You're a false meditator if you stay in solitude but lack discipline
You're a false friend if you don't help out
You're a false disciple if you ignore the words of your teacher.

Foolish habits and false ways, the list goes on.
Practice based on what I just said!

THIS SONG CONVINCED the student.

Rechungpa took a solemn vow that he would serve Milarepa, follow his advice, and practice hard. That night, he had a strange dream: he loaded a wool pack on a dog. "Write the words!" he shouted, and then he started walking towards a mountain. He reached the top, and suddenly eighty-eight men appeared from one side, and as many from the other side, the first as guides, the latter as hosts.

When Rechungpa asked Milarepa what the dream meant, the Jetsun sang this song:

The dog means you will have a friend
The wool shows your gentle nature
The words are a sign of your learning
Your shout "write!" means you will sing experience songs
The eighty-eight guides and hosts are just that: guides and
hosts.

BUT RECHUNGPA SOON had another intriguing dream: he was naked and stood in a stream, cleaning himself. Transformed into a bird, he

flew to a tree and looked into a mirror. Milarepa explained
Rechungpa's dream in a song:

> You'll throw off the layers of worldly concerns
> You'll bathe in the flawless instructions.
> Like a bird of love and compassion
> Flying with wings of merit and wisdom
> You'll land on the tree of enlightenment
> And the mirror will show you signs of dakinis.

A THIRD DREAM came to Rechungpa: a gem was shining on his head,
he had on a bright clean robe, and he was looking into a spotless
mirror. He held a vajra with his right hand and a skullcup full of
blood with his left. He sat cross-legged on a lotus, his back beaming
coils of light, his body in flames. Water sprang before his eyes, sun
and moon shone at his heart. Men and women in great numbers stood
to his left, while a sheep and a kid rested on his other side. Then the
sheep multiplied, and multiplied, and multiplied.

Hearing of this dream, Milarepa sang:

> The gem tells you to meditate on the Lama sitting on your
>   head
> The bright clean robe is the Kagyu lineage
> The spotless mirror, the ear-whispered transmission
> The vajra in your hand, your conquest over conceptual
>   thoughts
> The skullcup in your left hand, your experience of bliss and
>   emptiness.
>
> Sitting cross-legged means you abide in deep meditation
> Coils of light at your back symbolize your realization
> Experiences will spring like the water before you
> Your body will blaze with inner heat
> You'll abide in a luminous state as bright as sun and moon

You'll be guided by both women and men
The sheep and kid are the disciples under your care
They'll grow in numbers, your lineage will expand.

"AND THAT'S WHERE you're at," continued Milarepa, "so there's no more need for you to stay by my side. See, it's all about timing. You must go now, go and benefit beings." And Milarepa sang the song, Just Like That:

Listen Rechungpa, my son!
Know that conditions cause samsara or nirvana.
If you rely on your Lama
You'll hear his guidance just like that.

Listen Rechungpa, my son!
Don't be so attached to places.
If you meditate in natural retreats
Attainments will come just like that.

Basically, the cause of all evil
Is the grasping mind.
If you stop longing for things
You'll find happiness just like that.

Listen Rechungpa, my son!
Samsara's an endless cycle of rebirths.
Don't start a family, stay by yourself
The pure realm will rise just like that.

Listen Rechungpa, my son!
Now the dharma spreads, but many are corrupt.
Plenty of gurus, plenty of disciples—
But so much boast, babble and bad taste
Show them a pure transmission.

Listen Rechungpa, my son!
If you're sincere about practicing dharma,
Use it as the antidote to afflictive emotions.
Don't dazzle, don't deceive
And don't desire some kind of "heaven."

Listen Rechungpa, my son!
If you want enlightenment,
Stay off the pleasures of this life
Stay on the essence of mind
Stabilize your meditation. Do it!

"YOU USED TO GO places even when you should have stayed put," added
Milarepa. "But this time, you must go: start with the Jar Forest, by
the border of Do and Tibet. You'll help others there." And he sang
this song:

Rechungpa, you're like my first-born.
Now you leave me to go to Weu.

Meditate on the Lama on your head:
You hold all my transmissions, my son.

Guard well your samaya vow:
You carry the flame for this ear-whispered lineage.

Dispel the darkness of ignorance:
You have many disciples to guide.

Keep the teachings from the wrong ears:
You must plant well the tree of dharma.

Think of your lucky students:
Go now to the border down south.

Meditate in the Jar Forest,
You'll build a monastery between Do and Tibet.

RECHUNGPA PREPARED himself for departure. When all was ready, he
bowed before Milarepa and sang this song:

Father, your first-born, Rechungpa,
Goes to Tibet at your advice.
Rechungpa your son goes to Weu.
Bless me with your vajra body.
Keep me unhindered with your perfect words.
Guide my steps with your mind of no concepts.
Jetsun my father, be well.

Rechungpa your son goes to Weu.
Lead me, be kind to me.
You're a jewel, you're precious,
You're all the dimensions of enlightenment.
Jetsun protector, be well.

You're a magician, a clairvoyant,
Your have the eye of dharma.[54]
You clear the fog of ignorance.
How can I repay your kindness?
Jetsun, be well.

Meeting you has given me meaning.
You are powerful and great.
Jetsun my mentor, be well.

IT WAS TIME for Rechungpa to go. But Milarepa had a Final Song to
Rechungpa:

The view is non-partisan
Meditation is solitary

Conduct holds no villains
Samaya bridges appearances
Fruition is mindful of death
Do you get this?

"LISTEN CAREFULLY," MILAREPA added. "On the fourteenth day of the horse month in the year of the female wood hare, you must come back." Now Milarepa gave Rechungpa a large piece of gold. He also passed on many of his heart-teachings.

"I'll go because you want me to, but I can't stand leaving you Jetsun!" cried Rechungpa. Tears rolled down his face. "I'm going," he said between sobs, but still he sang another song:

The rivers of India and the rivers of Nepal
Flow their own way down their own valleys.
But rivers are rivers are water.
In the ocean they meet.

Around this earth that we inhabit
Sunrise is to the east, moonrise to the west.
But rays are rays are light.
On a cloudless eve they meet.

The minds of beings are ignorant,
The minds of the Buddhas are not.
But mind is mind is mind.
In the sphere of reality they meet.

Jetsun on the mountain, Rechungpa in the world,
We each follow our illusory way.
But dharma-body is dharma-body is us.
In the pure realm we meet.

Be well, Jetsun.
I'm leaving.

RECHUNGPA PLACED HIS HEAD at Milarepa's feet. He said more things still, prayers, wishes, hopes. Then he turned and left.

HE SETTLED FOR A WHILE in Jar Forest. One day, his old flame, Dembu, came to him asking for forgiveness. He wouldn't speak to her at first. But his friend Rinchen Drak talked him into seeing her. Rechungpa's heart softened. He let her come close, and studied her. She looked hard up, like she'd been through some rough times. Feeling terribly sorry, he broke down. Finally he put a gold nugget in her hands and sang her this song:

> I pray to you Milarepa, the greatest of them all.
> May I always remember your kindness,
> May you always hold me in your heart!
>
> You were a busy bee, Dembu, how you've changed!
> Do you remember our fight over the turquoise?
> I went back to my Lama,
> And there it was, on the mandala.
> I got goose bumps, I was amazed.
>
> My Lama first said, 'Don't you go to Weu!'
> But one day he said, 'Now you go to Weu!'
> It still strikes me as amazing.
>
> Look at the life of my father Jetsun:
> A piece of gold, a piece of rock, it's all the same to him.
> This gold that I gave you?
> He told me, 'Take it, take it!'
> It still strikes me as amazing.
>
> Now the gold is yours.
> It's to help you put up lots of Buddha statues—
> A form of physical purification.
> It's to help you recite mantras over and over—

A form of verbal purification.
It's to help you prepare tsatsas and shrines—
A form of mental purification.
Turn your senses on the mind within,
Meditate on the ear-whispered transmission
Pray again and again to the Jetsun.
Face your mistakes.
Try it, you'll attain great results.

RECHUNGPA FELT SO TOUCHED by Dembu that he took her under his care. He even cared for her uncle, a leper. He gave them teachings from the lineage and got them started on the path. The uncle was eventually cured of his leprosy. As for Dembu, she developed such realizations that she became an outstanding yogini greatly helpful to others.

NOTES

1 Dakini (*mkha 'gro ma*): lit. "sky-walker," a representation of primordial awareness. Wisdom dakinis are fully realized beings.

2 Samadhi (*tin nge 'dzin*): a state of intense meditative absorption.

3 Bodhichitta (*byang chub kyi sems*): lit. "mind of enlightenment," the aspiration to attain enlightenment in order to liberate all sentient beings from samsara.

4 The translator Marpa Lotsawa (*mar pa chos kyi blo gros* 1012-97): Milarepa's root Lama. Marpa studied Sanskrit and traveled three times to India in search of teachers. There, he met the great Naropa. He also received teachings from Atisha, Kukkuripa and others, and translated many texts from Sanskrit into Tibetan. See Trungpa, *Life of Marpa*.

5 Naropa (*na ro pa* 1016-1100): Indian Mahasiddha who left Nalanda University to study with Tilopa. Naropa was the teacher of Milarepa's root guru, Marpa. See Guenther, *Naropa*.

6 The generation and completion stages are phases in tantric meditation: the generation stage (T. *bskyed rim*, Skt. *utpattikrama*) consists of transforming one's ordinary perceptions into a tantric experience whereby all sound is the mantra of the deity being practiced, all form, the body of the deity and all thought, the wisdom of the deity; in the completion stage (T. *rdzogs rim*, Skt. *sampannakrama*), the yogi dissolves

the visualization and rests in the natural state. See Jamgon Kongtrul, *Creation and Completion.*

7 Relatively little is known of the Mahasiddha Saraha. He came from a Brahmin background but acted in ways outside his caste, drinking and consorting with an arrowsmith's daughter. He probably lived in the 8th-9th centuries (Dowman, *Masters of Mahamudra*, 72), and taught Shavaripa. Saraha is best known for his three Dohas, or Songs, to the King, Queen and People. See Guenther, *Saraha.*

8 Dharma-body (*chos kyi sku*): the basic space-like nature of reality, one of three bodies of enlightenment. See note 13.

9 *Yidam* deity (*yi dam*): a personal meditation deity.

10 *Samaya* commitments (T. *dam tshig*, Skt. samaya): commitments in tantric practice ranging from keeping harmony with one's Lama and fellow practitioners to pursuing one's practice with consistency.

11 Inner heat, or *tummo* (*gtum mo*): the fierce internal warmth generated through a special meditation practice.

12 Five faculties (T. *dbang po lnga*, Skt. *pancendriya*): faith (T. *dad pa*, Skt. *sraddha*); perseverance (T. *brtson 'grus*, Skt. *virya*); mindfulness (T. *dran pa*, Skt. *smrti*); contemplation (T. *ting nge 'dzin*, Skt. *samadhi*); and wisdom (T. *shes rab*, Skt. *prajna*).

13 The dimensions or bodies of enlightenment (T. *sku*, Skt. *kaya*): a realized being has three modes of being—the dharma-body (T. *chos kyi sku*, Skt. *dharmakaya*), which is the space-like nature of all phenomena that does not arise, does not abide, does not go out of existence. From the realization of the dharma-body arises the enlightened enjoyment body (T. *longs spyod rdzogs pa'i sku*, Skt. *sambogakaya*), perceived only by bodhisattvas. This in turn gives rise to the enlightened emanation body (T. *sprul pa'i sku*, Skt. *nirmanakaya*), perceived by all beings. The union of these three bodies is the essential body (T. *ngo bo nyid sku*, Skt. *svabhavikakaya*).

14 Reality itself (T. *chos nyid*, Skt. *dharmata*): the ultimate nature of mind and phenomena, emptiness beyond concepts.

15 The four yogas (*rnal 'byor bzhi*) are stages of Mahamudra meditation

within the Kagyu tradition: one-pointedness (*rtse gcig*) means resting in the nature of mind in the present moment; simplicity, or freedom-from-elaboration (*spros bral*) is the dawning realization of emptiness; one-taste (*ro gcig*) is the direct knowing of mind and phenomena as being of one nature; and non-meditation (*sgom med*) refers to the stable realization that there is no difference between appearances and emptiness.

16 The perfections (T. *pha rol tu phyin pa*, Skt. *paramita*) mark the path to enlightenment. The Prajnaparamita Sutra gives six perfections, but four are sometimes added beyond the first six to make ten perfections: generosity (T. *sbyin*, Skt. *dana*); ethics (T. *tshul khrims*, Skt. *shila*); patience (T. *bzod pa*, Skt. *ksanti*); diligence or perseverance (T. *brtson 'grus*, Skt. *virya*); meditative concentration (T. *bsam gten*, Skt. *dhyana*); wisdom (T. *shes rab*, Skt. *prajna*); skillful means (T. *thabs*, Skt. *upaya*); aspiration (T. *smon lam*, Skt. *pranidhana*); power (T. *stobs*, Skt. *bala*); and primordial awareness (T. *ye shes*, Skt. *jnana*). Ordinary generosity is valuable, but it becomes the "perfection of generosity" when it is accompanied by the wisdom that realizes emptiness, and likewise for the others.

17 Mahayana, or the great vehicle (*theg pa chen po*): the bodhisattva path endowed with the compassionate intention not to pass into nirvana until all beings are liberated. Tantra, or the diamond vehicle (T. *rdo rje theg pa*, Skt. *vajrayana*) shares the same Mahayana intention and includes powerful mantra recitations, visualizations and yogic practices that emphasize the state of natural liberation already present in all of existence.

18 Mother and child reuniting: in this context, "mother" is a code word for one's Buddha nature, while "child" is the recognition of what one's teacher has pointed out.

19 Vajrayogini (*rdo rje rnal 'byor ma*): female meditation deity of the mother class of Anuttarayoga tantra. See English, *Vajrayogini*.

20 The six realms (*rigs drug*) are the six basic states for sentient beings: gods; demi-gods; humans; animals; hungry ghosts; and hell beings.

21 "Mandate" is a free translation for *phyogs*, lit. "direction."

22 "Consciousness' conditioning" is a free translation for *tshogs drug rkyen snang stong pa'i ngang,* lit. "in the state of emptiness of the conditions of the six consciousnesses and their objects."

23 "I *am* Mahamudra," sings Milarepa. Mahamudra is a series of practices leading to a direct understanding of the nature of mind and reality—ultimately the absence of inherent existence, which pervades all phenomena. As Maitripa says, "[Mahamudra] doesn't have an identity to show / For that reason, the nature of mind / Is itself the very state of Mahamudra." (My translation from the Tibetan *rang gi ngo bo bstan du med / de phyir sems kyi rang bzhin nyid / phyag rgya chen po'i ngang nyid las*). Source: *Do ha mDzod brGyad,* Rumtek, Sikkhim.

24 One of four seals, or four mudras (T. *phyag rgya bzhi,* Skt. *catumudra*): samaya mudra (*dam tshig phyag rgya*); dharma mudra (*chos kyi phyag rgya*); karmamudra (*las kyi phyag rgya*); and mahamudra or shunyata mudra (*tsong pa'i phyag rgya*). Karmamudra refers to the consort in tantric practice. In the lower tantras (Kriya, Carya, Yoga) karmamudra is a ritual hand gesture.

25 *Torma* offerings (*gtor ma*): ritualized food offerings usually in the shape of a cone.

26 Two accumulations (T. *tshogs gnyis,* Skt. *sambharadvaya*): accumulation of merit (T. *bsod nams tshogs,* Skt. *punysambhara*) through positive activities undertaken with a pure motivation; and accumulation of wisdom (T. *ye shes tshogs,* Skt. *jnanasambhara*) through realization of emptiness.

27 Four immeasurables (*tshad med bzhi*): immeasurable love (*byams pa tshad med*); immeasurable compassion (*snying rje tshad med*); immeasurable joy (*dga' ba tshad med*); and immeasurable equanimity (*btang snyoms tshad med*).

28 Six medicinal plants (*bzang drug*): nutmeg; clover; saffron; big cardamon; small cardamon; and bamboo pitch.

29 Eight worldly concerns (*chos brgyad*): attachments and aversions to mundane issues that a practitioner is advised to set aside: attachment to gain; fame; praise; and pleasure. And aversion to loss; infamy; blame; and pain.

30 Tetralemma (T. *mu bzhi*, Skt. *catuskoti*): a relationship between two objects or sets of objects (say A and B) that considers four possibilities: that which is only A but not B; that which is only B but not A; that which is both A and B; and that which is neither A nor B.

31 Mount Kailash in far-west Tibet, referred to in the text by its informal name, Mount Ti-se (*ti se*), long regarded as the *axis mundi* by Buddhists and other spiritual traditions. Gyurme Dorje, *Tibet Handbook*, 336.

32 Tantric Mahayana, see note 17.

33 The four opponent powers (*stobs bzhi*) are steps to counteract negative deeds: sincere regret; refuge; remedial actions and practices; and a vow not to repeat the deed again.

34 Six Yogas (*rnal 'byor drug*): referring here to the Six Yogas of Naropa, powerful techniques using the body's energy to realize the nature of mind: inner heat (*gtum mo*); illusory body (*sgyu lus*); dream yoga (*rmi lam*); clear light yoga (*'od gsal*); transference of consciousness (*'pho ba*); and yoga of the bardo (*bar do*).

35 Tara (*sgrol ma*): female meditation deity greatly beloved in Tibet. Known as the Saviouress, Tara attained complete enlightenment and vowed to remain in samsara to guide all beings to liberation. See Bokar Rinpoche, *Tara*.

36 Vajradhara Buddha (*rdo rje 'chang*): lit. "vajra holder," Vajradhara represents the essence of an enlightened state, the union of wisdom and compassion.

37 Tilopa (*ti lo pa*, 988-1069): a Brahmin by background, Tilopa turned to the tantric Buddhist masters Saraha, Nagarjuna and Matangi among others. After more than a decade of intense practice, he attained realization and received directly from Vajradhara the transmission which, from then on, has been passed from master to disciple in the Kagyu lineage. His principal disciple was Naropa. See Marpa, *Tilopa*.

38 Six supernormal powers (*mngon shes drug*): miraculous powers (*rdzu 'phrul gyi bya ba shes pa'i mngon shes*); mind reading (*pha rol gyi sems shes pa'i mngon shes*); clairaudience (*lha'i rna ba'i mngon shes*); clairvoyance (*lha'i mig gi mngon shes*); knowledge of past lives (*sngon gyi gnas rjes su*

dran pa'i mngon shes); and exhaustion of impurities (*zag pa zad pa'i mngon shes*).

39 Ten perfections, see note 16.

40 This line refers to victory over the four evils (*bdud bzhi*) which are challenges to overcome before attaining enlightenment: the evil of aggregates (misconceiving the aggregates as inherently existing); afflictive emotions (being confused by afflictive emotions); death (having one's practice interrupted by death); god-child (being distracted by sensual pleasure).

41 In different songs, Milarepa articulates the views of different Buddhist schools. Here, the meaning can be understood from the perspective of the Empty-of-Other, or Shentong school (*gzhan stong*), which is based on sutras on Buddha nature and the *Uttaratantra* (*rgyud bla ma*). Jamgon Kongtrul posits the two truths according to the Empty-of-Other school as follows: "The imputed nature and the dependent nature are the relative truth; the ultimate truth is the perfectly present, self-aware primordial wisdom." (My translation from the Tibetan *kun brtags gzhan dbang kun rdzob don dam ni / yongs grub rang rig ye shes gzhan stong lugs*, Jamgon Kongtrul, *Gaining Certainty*, 16). For a study of Buddha nature and the Empty-of-Other school, see Stearns, *The Buddha from Dolpo*; and Jamgon Kongtrul, *Buddha Nature*.

42 See chapter thirteen, "To a Scholar."

43 Gampopa (*sgam po pa*, 1079-1153): also known as Dakpo Lhaje, the Physician from Lhaje, Gampopa transmitted the Kadampa lineage, received from Atisha, and the Mahamudra tradition, received from Milarepa. Founder of the Dakpo Kagyu tradition, he wrote *The Jewel Ornament of Liberation*, which lays out the stages on the path. See Stewart, *Gampopa*.

44 See chapter ten, "You Want to Argue?"

45 Three higher trainings (T. *bslab pa gsum*, Skt. *trisika*): ethical conduct; meditative concentration; and discriminating awareness.

46 *Emaho!* lit. "wondrous!" expresses the joyful discovery of the natural state already perfect and liberated, as Milarepa explains in his song.

47 *Tsatsas* (*tsha tsha*): miniature clay replicas of deities or stupas.

48 "Feeding a glutton" is a free translation for *kha lan ston mo'i re mos 'dra*, lit. "paying back a series of feasts."

49 Maitripa studied at Nalanda, was a disciple of Shavaripa, and transmitted Maitreya's *Uttaratantra Shastra* as well as other teachings to Marpa, Milarepa's Lama. He lived in the 11th century, but the historiography is complicated by the fact that Maitripa appears to be sometimes referred to as the Mahasiddha Avadhutipa (Dowman, *Masters of Mahamudra*, 244).

50 This is the famous Padampa Sangye (*pha dam pa sang rgyas*, 1020-1100) from India, who brought the *Pacifying*, or *Zhije* (*zhi byed*) tradition to Tibet. His principal disciple was the yogini Machik Labdron.

51 *PHET!* This expletive aims to startle the practitioner who can use the moment of surprise to look at who, or what, was just jolted by the sound.

52 Four classes of tantra (*rgyud sde bzhi*): Kriya tantra (*bya ba'i rgyud*); Carya tantra (*spyod pa'i rgyud*); Yoga tantra (*rnal 'byor rgyud*); and Anuttarayoga tantra (*med pa'i rgyud*).

53 Chenrezig (T. *spyan ras gzigs*, Skt. *Avalokiteshvara*): the deity of compassion. See Bokar Rinpoche, *Chenrezig.*

54 One of five eyes (*spyan lnga*) possessed by enlightened beings: divine eye (*lha'i spyan*); fleshy eye (*sha'i spyan*); wisdom eye (*shes rab kyi spyan*); eye of dharma (*chos kyi spyan*); and eye of primordial awareness (*ye shes kyi spyan*).

BIBLIOGRAPHY

Bokar Rinpoche, 1991. *Chenrezig, Lord of Love*. Trans. from French by Christiane Buchet. San Francisco: Clear Point Press.

———,1999. *Tara: The Feminine Divine*. San Francisco: Clear Point Press.

Chang, Garma C.C., transl., 1999. *The Hundred Thousand Songs of Milarepa*. Repr. Boston: Shambhala Publications.

Conze, Edward, 1985. *The Large Sutra on Perfect Wisdom with the Divisions of the Abhisamayalankara*. Repr. Berkeley: University of California Press.

Dowman, Keith, 1985. *Masters of Mahamudra*. Albany: State University of New York Press.

English, Elizabeth, 2002. *Vajrayogini: Her Visualizations, Rituals and Forms*. Boston: Wisdom Publications.

Evans-Wentz, W.Y., 1969. *Tibet's Great Yogi Milarepa*. 2d ed. London: Oxford University Press.

Guenther, Herbert, 1993. *Ecstatic Spontaneity: Saraha's Three Cycles of Doha*. Fremont, CA: Asian Humanities Press.

———, 1995. *The Life and Teaching of Naropa*. Repr. Boston: Shambhala Publications.

Gyurme Dorje, 1999. *Tibet Handbook*. 2d ed. Bath, England: Footprint Handbooks.

Jamgon Kongtrul, 1996. *Creation and Completion*. Trans. Sarah Harding. Boston: Wisdom Publications.

———, 1997. *Gaining Certainty about the Provisional and Definitive Meanings* . Trans. Anne Burchardi and Ari Goldfield. Kathmandu: Marpa Institute for Translation.

——— and Khenpo Tsultrim Gyamtso Rinpoche and Rosemary Fuchs,

2000. *Buddha Nature: The Mahayana Uttaratantra Shastra with Commentary.* Ithaca, N.Y.: Snow Lion Publications.

Kelsang Gyatso, Geshe, 1996. *Guide to Dakini Land: The Highest Yoga Tantra Practice of Buddha Vajrayogini.* London: Tharpa Publications.

Kunga Rimpoche, Lama, and Brian Cutillo, trans., 1978. *Drinking the Mountain Stream.* Novato, CA: Lotsawa.

——, 1978. *Miraculous Journeys: New Stories and Songs by Milarepa.* Novato, CA: Lotsawa.

Mar-pa Chos-kyi bLo-gros, 1995. *The Life of the Mahasiddha Tilopa.* Trans. Fabrizio Torricelli and Acharya Sangya T. Naga. Ed. Vyvyan Cayley. Dharamsala: Library of Tibetan Works and Archives.

Mullin, Glenn, 1997. *Readings on the Six Yogas of Naropa.* Ithaca, N.Y.: Snow Lion Publications.

Riggs, Nicole, 2001. *Like An Illusion: Lives of the Shangpa Kagyu Masters.* Eugene: Dharma Cloud Press.

Stearns, Cyrus, 1989. *The Buddha from Dolpo.* Albany: State University of New York Press.

Stewart, Jampa Mackenzie, 1995. *The Life of Gampopa: The Incomparable Dharma Lord of Tibet.* Ithaca, N.Y.: Snow Lion Publications.

Takpo Tashi Namgyal, 1986. *Mahamudra: The Quintessence of Mind and Meditation.* Trans. Lobsang P. Lhalungpa. Boston: Shambhala Publications.

Trungpa, Chogyam, 1987. *Cutting Through Spiritual Materialism.* Repr. Boston: Shambhala Publications.

——, 1994. *Illusion's Game: The Life and Teaching of Naropa.* Repr. Ed. Sherab Chodzin. Boston: Shambhala Publications.

—— and Nalanda Translation Committee, 1995. *The Life of Marpa the Translator: Seeing Accomplishes All.* Repr. Boston: Shambhala Publications.

Tsultrim Gyamtso Rinpoche, Khenpo, 1986. *Progressive Stages of Meditation on Emptiness.* 2d ed. Trans. Shenpen Hookham. Oxford: Longchen Foundation.

Wilson, Martin, ed., 1996. *In Praise of Tara: Songs to the Saviouress: Source Texts from India and Tibet on Buddhism's Great Goddess.* 2d ed. Boston: Wisdom Publications.

INDEX